Why Lazarus Laughed

Also by Wei Wu Wei

Why Lazarus Laughed

The Essential Doctrine, Zen - Advaita - Tantra

WEI WU WEI

SENTIENT PUBLICATIONS, LLC

First Sentient Publications edition, 2003

Copyright © 2003 by Kegan Paul Limited.
Reprinted in the United States by Sentient Publications, by
arrangement with Kegan Paul Limited, London.

Grateful acknowledgment is made for permission to use
Matt Errey's editorial notes.

Printed in the United States of America

Cover design by Kim Johansen, Black Dog Design
Book design by Anna Bergstrom

Library of Congress Cataloging-in-Publication Data

Wei, Wu Wei.
 Why Lazarus laughed : the essential doctrine Zen--Advaita--
Tantra.--1st ed.
  p. cm.
 Includes index.
 ISBN 1-59181-011-6
1. Asia—Religion. 2. Philosophy, Asian. 3. Advaita. I. Title.
BL1033 .W45 2003
202--dc22

2003016343

SENTIENT PUBLICATIONS
A Limited Liability Company
1113 Spruce St.
Boulder, CO 80302
www.sentientpublications.com

*Living
Should Be
Perpetual and Universal
Benediction.*

Contents

The Title of This Book

Titles of books are sometimes indications only. Here for instance, there is not really any doctrine, but just reflections of the moon in a puddle. And quite certainly there is no teacher. Essential understanding, however, might have found its way into occasional pages—whether understood or not by the transmitter is beside the point.

Under the title of this book only three religions are cited, those that are formally non-dualist. But this apparent limitation does not imply that such is not also the essential "doctrine" of the three Semitic faiths, Judaism, Christianity and Islam, which are formally dualist, and whose esoteric aspects are Kabala, Gnosis and Sufism.

In Christianity the dualism of Creator and created is resolved in what is implied by Godhead, but this is not developed in the theology, moreover the recorded words of Jesus are few and are chiefly addressed to the simple-minded, and the esoteric doctrine was cast out by the council of Constantinople in A.D. 553. Therefore the Christian evidence chiefly resides in Gnostic records that are little known, in the early Fathers, and in sages and saints such as Meister Eckhart and St. John of the Cross, who were obliged by the dogmas of the Church to cloak the non-dualism which is implicit in their realisation of the truth. For this reason it is unpractical to use Christian evidence in such a collection of observations as this.

It seems unlikely that anything but the superficial teaching of Jesus, that which he taught in parables "so that they should *not* understand," has been available to the "Christian" public since the excommunication of Origen in A.D. 553, three hundred years after he wrote his works.

However, in view of the tidal-wave of interest in metaphysics which reveals a considerable percentage of modern man as being driven to seek the truth concerning himself and the universe, it seems inevitable that the day will arrive when the doctrines of Iesous Christos will once more be revealed to mankind.

I have not mentioned Tao? That which is understood does not need statement. The doctrine of Tao is an implicit rather than an explicit doctrine. The doctrine of Tao is itself the essential doctrine. This little book might have been called Tao—were not such a title presumptuous.

In general, capital letters have been used when the term implies that which is unique. When the same word is written with a lower-case letter multiplicity is implied.

Preface

This work, like *Fingers Pointing Towards the Moon*, is a series of observations on the path of a pilgrim, and represents a continual development of the intuitions and ideas so experienced.

Therefore at no point is a final statement of doctrine to be sought, which would indeed be dogma, and which this could never be.

In this process later observations correct, supplement and achieve earlier ones, perhaps contradict them in certain details. Nowhere is absolute truth to be expected. Nowhere is anyone asked to believe. Nowhere is there finality to be found.

A pilgrim shares the fruit he has gathered by the wayside—that is all.

It may be observed, even perhaps objected, that this later volume is increasingly concerned with two or three themes only. The inference should be clear: as the wayfarer proceeds, the broad base of the mountain is left behind, the path narrows and the multitudinous objects of apparent interest that abound at the lower levels merge into a few essential ones that ultimately will become one only—as may be observed in the concentrated teaching of those who arrived at the summit, such as Huang Po, Padma Sambhava and Ramana Maharshi. Were it not so even here the work could hardly be genuine or that little it professes to be.

Thereafter there are no further problems, for subsidiary

ones are derivative, and ultimately there is nothing further to be said.

All that remains is the catalystic understanding of that ultimate problem that the long wayfaring has revealed.

—W.W.W.

Prolegomenon

The normal occidental, brought up in quasi-absolute materialism, whose religion—in so far as he has any—is dualistic (which comports the opposition of spirit and matter, of God and man), usually believes that nothing exists except that which his senses can perceive, i.e. in a universe confined within the limitations of his sensorial apparatus. Such a man cannot possibly comprehend that reality expounded by the Sages, without a complete reversal of all his beliefs, a total revaluation of all his values.

Such a transformation is only possible to a few, and it cannot reasonably occur within a period less than a considerable number of years. Even so it requires a powerful urge from the plane of reality, which few experience, and an intellectual apparatus of an order that is sparsely distributed in any society.

Moreover, no organised system of re-education to that end exists in the West, and years are apt to pass before such a man even begins to realise that what he believes to be reality is phenomenal, and that what he believes to be phenomenal may be Reality.

And by then he has found out that the phenomenal universe appears to exist precisely because his sensorial apparatus has interpreted reality in that form, and is in fact a product of mind.

And that is not where the journey ends, but the terminus from which the traveller sets forth, for, in order that intuition may penetrate effectively, it needs a mind that is conditioned to interpret it.

Why Lazarus Laughed

WORK AND PLAY

1 ·~ Revaluation of Values: Three False Values

1. Karma ("Action") must surely be active, not passive. It is not ours, rather we are its. We are corks in a turbulent eddying stream of karma; karma is the force-field to which we are subject on the plane of phenomena.

2. The "I," "Me," "Self," whatever term we encounter or use to describe our reality, is misleading. All these terms suggest a being, yet the Buddha stated again and again in the Diamond Sutra that there is no such being.

Our reality is a state, *l'etat sans ego,* a *state* not a *person*, the I-less state. It is always present, and it alone is present.

3. The "me," "ego," "self," "personality," the personal pronoun "I" as we use it every moment in thought and word, is just a mistake, an error of judgement, like a shadow mistaken for its substance on a moonlight night. Though there could be no shadow if there were no substance, nevertheless the shadow remains unreal (unsubstantial)—and when the moon is hidden by a cloud the shadow no longer exists.

Every time we say "I" we are making a mistake, mistaking something that isn't there for something that is. Every such time the I-less state has been misinterpreted as something personal.

If we were to perceive the shadow as such, and thereby recognise its substance, the I-less state for what it is, the whole "cave of illusions" would collapse and vanish for ever. Reality would lie naked before us—and we should be it.

Yet expression of the I-less state takes the form "I am" on the plane of dualism, but no qualification is possible: it is the "I am that I am" of the Bible which may be described as a

1

personal expression of the Impersonal. Rather is it just "Am," i.e. Consciousness.

REALITY AND MANIFESTATION

2 · Buddhas for Burning

I think we have understood that dogmas in a world of constant mutation are necessarily false? And since we know that everything we formulate in words, that is, seen dualistically, is inevitably deformed, we can readily understand that all doctrines, religious, philosophical, scientific, cannot represent more than a reflection of truth.

Men and women who seek doctrines, study them, endeavour to follow them, are impeding their own progress. The Masters, from the Buddha down, in their frequent condemnation of "discoursing" have made that clear, and in declaring that there must be no attachment to, or identification with, the *Dharma* itself (or any *dharma*), that even the teaching of the Buddha himself must be discarded, have left no room for doubt on that score.

Doctrines, scriptures, sutras, essays, are not to be regarded as systems to be followed. They merely contribute to understanding. They should be for us a source of stimulation, and nothing more.

We must create each his own *dharma*, understanding, and may use those of others to help us to that end; they have no other value for us. Adopted, rather than used as a stimulus, they are a hindrance. As the Zen master stated to the monk whom he found studying a sutra, "Do not let the sutra upset you—upset the sutra yourself instead." Some Masters expressed themselves more forcibly, as when they recommended that Buddhas (statues of) were for burning and on a cold day used one as firewood, and in advising, "If you meet the Buddha, turn aside and look the other way." Such statements shock the sense of reverence inculcated by the devotional religions, but their meaning, their aim, their importance, are evident.

PHYSICS AND METAPHYSICS

3 ⸱⁓ Man Is a River

A river has a name, a character, a personality; it is liked or disliked as an entity. This is due to a variety of factors: its rapidity or sluggishness, its breadth, depth, length, its form and course, its smoothness, number of islands, and the vegetation and topographical character of its immediate environment. But it flows; from whatever angle you may look, it is never the same for two consecutive seconds. It is just passing water, each ripple, each drop, resembling its predecessor and its successor but never the same ripple or drop.

There is no river. There is no man.

TIME AND SPACE

4 ⸱⁓ Time and Movement Are Two Aspects of a Single Phenomenon

Portrait of a Gentleman

We are vortices whose centre is a point that is motionless and eternal but which appears in manifestation as motion which increases in velocity in the manner of a whirlpool or tornado (whose epicentre is still) from nucleus to periphery.

But the nucleus is in Reality, whereas the vortex is phenomenon in the form of a multi-dimensional force-field.

The periphery of this force-field appears as matter, of various densities, extended in space and moving in time at divers velocities.

The totality of this appearance partakes of the consciousness which is its core and only reality.

5 – Living Backwards

What we know as Time is the only manner in which our psycho-somatic apparatus is able to interpret the fourth dimension of the space in which we live phenomenally, and we interpret it serially, lineally, as one-thing-after-another. But there is no apparent reason why that lineal interpretation should proceed in one direction only, nor any apparent likelihood that it does. In consciousness it might be expected to proceed in one lineal direction, in the unconscious in the other, whereas in abnormal conditions, such as near-death by suffocation or accident, our "time-apparatus" sometimes re-registers the whole of our life-experience in a composite flash.

❧

Is it not probable that we live our lives both "forwards" and "backwards" (two arbitrary evaluations) simultaneously? Need we look further for an explanation of foresight, second-sight, precognition, premonitory dreams and all the other not-so-great mysteries?

❧

In which direction of Time do we live in our dreams? Is their reinterpretation by waking consciousness in its own time-sequence not the most probable explanation of their oddity? Is there then any mystery in a dream whose action leads up to a "noise" that awakens us at the moment it actually occurs in the next room?

❧

Is there any reason to doubt that our dreaming mind functions uninterruptedly throughout the twenty-four hours of our time, that is, from birth, or before it, to death? To what extent it is subjected to a time-sequence may be doubtful and in which direction such time-sequence may flow, but it is likely to enjoy a greater freedom in that respect than does our waking consciousness.

THE EGO

6 ·— *Policemen Disguising Themselves as Thieves in Order to Catch Themselves*

Of the many earnest, and how earnest, people we may observe reading, attending lectures, studying and practising disciplines, devoting their energies to the attainment of a liberation which is by definition unattainable, how many are *not* striving *via the ego-concept* which is itself the only barrier between what they think they are and that which they wish to become but always have been and always will be?

Were we to read less and understand more might we not

remember that the T'ang Masters repeatedly told us that mind cannot be reached through mind, and that there is only one mind? Perhaps less earnest people pay more attention to what they were told by those who KNEW?

Armchair Travelling

Knowing that no such thing as an "ego" can exist, but continuing to talk and think about "the" ego, i.e. as something still believed in, is like someone who decides to go for a journey, packs his luggage—and then never leaves home!

7 ⸱- *Le Fantoche*

If one seeks to rid oneself of, or even to transcend, a false self, ego, or personality, one thereby accepts as a fact the existence of such entity and so-doing affirms its stranglehold (a constraint can be real or imaginary—such as that of the chicken's beak held by a chalk-line).

That of which we need to rid ourselves, to transcend, is the false concept whereby we assume that entity's existence. We have only to look with penetration in order to perceive that there is in fact nothing in us which corresponds to the concept of an entity, in our ever-changing kaleidoscope of electronic impulses interpreted in the false perspective of a time-sequence. A pulsating force-field is not an entity to be transcended, any more than is vapour issuing from the spout of a kettle, or the apparently living being resulting from the rapid and consecutive projection of isolated and motionless "stills" (or quanta) on to a cinematograph screen.

There is not, there could not be, any entity; the Buddha based his doctrine upon that realisation; there can be nothing of which to rid ourselves, or to transcend, except an erroneous concept. . . .

REALITY AND MANIFESTATION

8 ⁓ Free-will Versus Determinism

Discussions concerning the predominance of the will over destiny, or vice versa, can only take place among those who lack knowledge of the root of both. Those who have knowledge of the Self, sole root of the will and of destiny, are free from the one and the other.
After that how can they take part in such discussions?
RAMANA MAHARSHI ULLADU NARPADU
Forty Verses on the Knowledge of Being, 19

An essential difference between a Jivan Mukta and an ordinary unenlightened man is that the former has transcended the duality inherent in that apparent contradiction of between Free-will and Determinism.

The Jivan Mukta, having abandoned the concept of an ego, subject to which the ordinary man lives, his will no longer has any alternative to complete harmony with that of the cosmic order, so that he "wills" what must be, without any kind of resistance (there being in him no longer any psychic mechanism capable of resistance), whereas the ordinary man, subject to his ego-concept, is unable to perceive what must be, and seeks to substitute the desires aggregated to his artificial "ego," which he imagines he is free to fulfill if he can.

Neither is "free" in the sense thought of by the ordinary man, but the one experiences no lack of "freedom" or any constraint, whereas the other spends his life in an imaginary

7

conflict, a tilting against wind-mills, trying to assert a "freedom" he could not possibly enjoy.

That is why the Jivan Mukta lives his life without conflict, and usually devotes himself to helping the unenlightened to rid themselves of their errors by transcending the ego-concept, for on that plane, the plane of understanding, real understanding being in a further dimension that is not subject to the Space-Time mechanism, even the ordinary man is "free" (of the aforesaid mechanicity) to rid himself of his ignorance.

9 ·— Free-will - I

Our sole freedom is the faculty of understanding, for there is only one mind, and nothing else is. (The T'ang Masters have been quoted to this effect, especially Hsi Yun.)

It follows that our only liberty of "action" lies in the exercise of this faculty, and the resulting change in our apparent selves.

If this should appear difficult to comprehend we might do well to envisage mind as an ultimate subtlety or essence traversing all dimensions, manifesting in all, and constituting thereby a *liaison* between the densest force-field of the material world and Absolute Reality, of which it is the purest manifestation perceptible to us.

Free-will - II

How can a figment of the imagination have any effect on anything that is not itself a figment of the imagination? Therefore any effect resulting from an act of "will" subject to the ego-concept can only be as imaginary as itself.

10 ·- Freedom - I

Our freedom resides in mind, of which "ours" is the aspect we experience. Knowledge is unreal, or relative, but Understanding is real. We are free to understand if we can.

But knowledge comes by reasoning, whereas understanding comes by intuition. It may be, however, that the knowledge obtained by reasoning can open the way for intuition, though to that end knowledge must be seen for what it is, that it is relative and not real.

As a result of understanding we function on a different plane, little as it may effect the mode of life we enjoy. Above all we may come to perceive the futility of our struggle to impose the supposed desires of our "ego" on the inevitable. The Taoist injunction, taken over by Buddhism, to live in accordance with "nature" must mean just that.

Freedom - II

The Maharshi also wrote on a piece of paper when a young man: "Whatever is destined not to happen will not happen, try as you may. Whatever is destined to happen will happen, do what you may to prevent it. This is certain."

He was uncompromising in his teaching. His answer was: "Find out who it is who is predestined or has free-will." More explicitly he said: "All the actions that the body is to perform are already decided upon at the time it comes into existence: the only freedom you have is whether or not to identify yourself with the body." That means that in playing our part in the comedy in which we are given a role and which we call our life, we can identify ourselves with our role, really imagine we are the character whose part we are playing, or stand apart mentally and play it by sheer technique.

"All the actions *the body is to perform* are already decided upon at the time it comes into existence. . . ." The mind has a certain freedom, but not to decide the actions of the body. Its most valuable freedom is the liberty to understand and thereby to rid itself of its identifications and particularly of its illusion of individuality. When it has understood as much as that, it is at the disposition of Mind Itself and may awaken to Reality at any moment.

11 · Débris - I

There may well be "dog" (in Reality), but there cannot be such a thing as a dog.

☙

What justification could there be for regarding the bodies of living things as having any higher value, or nobler purpose, than that of prospective manure? According to what law is there any higher?

☙

Play your part in the comedy, but don't identify yourself with your role!

Manifestations of multiple energies, what else are men?

Karma is not a thing-in-itself nor a system invented by some esoteric religion. "Karma" is a short and convenient word for the cumbrous expression "the force of circumstances."

We are all aspects of one another.

Blaming a man for what he "does" is in accordance with the same process of logic as blaming a door when it bangs or an object when it falls on your foot.

☙

A school is an efficient instrument for reinforcing the stranglehold of the so-called "ego."

Much reading is also a struggling to "attain."

12 ·~ Turning the Other Cheek

That was something that particular force-field had to do. What a clown I would be to praise or blame that force-field on account of it—as though it were an act of free-will on the part of an independent entity! The Self of which that force-field is a manifestation is immutable and does not "act." Neither the reality of that force-field or of this one is involved. Were I even to smile at the incident, that would indicate that I still retained some trace of the notion that an individual entity "did" something that pleased or annoyed me.

Poached Eggs (all of us)

Arguing about transcending the I-concept, "reducing" the "power" of the ego, or what-not, is merely evidence of continued belief in the reality of that which, being merely a concept, is totally unreal.

It is like a man saying, "I am perfectly sane: I know that I am not a poached egg, instead I am busily engaged in unpoaching myself and soon I shall not even need a piece of toast in order to be able to sit down."

❧

Have we ever wondered why the Zen Masters, on the rare occasions on which they refer to the I-concept, only do so indirectly in some such terms as "the dirt on your face"?

It is enough for them to show us that concepts are inevitably unreal. Any attempt to "reduce" or "transcend" or "discipline" what is only a concept can only affirm its illusory appearance of reality. When all concepts are seen for what they are, that is, are recognised as such and nothing more, the ego finds itself in the waste-paper basket with the rest.

❧

From the "Physics and Metaphysics" angle of vision we have seen clearly enough that there could not possibly be such a thing as an I. The notion is as ludicrous as attributing individuality to the sound made by reeds stirred by the wind.

WORK AND PLAY

13 ·~ Group Egoism—A Causerie

We worry a lot about the I-concept of the individual, but rarely about the I-concept of the group. Families also sometimes have developed protuberant egos. And as for nations. . . .

Nationalism is a manifestation of the ego of a group, often exacerbated to an extent that social conditions deny to the individual.

Even associations, clubs, and particularly political parties, develop an I-concept with the lamentable and ridiculous results that accompany all manifestations of this concept.

Yet there is no reality in such phenomena, other than the ultimate reality without which phenomena could not manifest.

But just as there have always been families which have escaped the development of such a concept, and associations, clubs, even parties which are merely SUCH, so nationalism is only a sporadic growth and has not always existed in our or any other civilisation.

Many people are proud of this manifestation and regard it as a virtue, just as some people cherish pride as a virtue: *les primaires civilisés, les civilisés primaires.*

Perhaps if we are able to transcend the ego-ism of the group we may the more easily find the way to transcend the ego-ism of the individual, for one and all are identical concepts and, one and all, devoid of reality.

PHYSICS AND METAPHYSICS

14 ·— Travail

Anthropologists, and even the general public, know that in many parts of the world, among some so-called primitive peoples, the husband goes to bed and experiences the birth-pains of his wife who is in travail.

It would be of no avail were you to tell him that his pains are imaginary, that he had no organs susceptible of causing such pains, and that he has no occasion to have them. He is subjected to that concept and is unable to transcend it.

Is not the I-concept, to which we, so-called non-primitive people, are subjected, just that?

Dream Figures. "As Below . . ."

It may be useful to re-emphasise that not only the protagonists but everyone who appears in our dreams is the dreamer of the dream. This should be obvious enough, but until thought of and tested it is apt to be denied. Whatever name and apparent identity is attributed to dream personages, it can readily be perceived, not merely theoretically, that such persons are not in fact the individuals named as they were or are, even in memory, but the projection on to those names of a concept of the dreaming mind utilising just sufficient traits drawn from memory to give some verisimilitude to the attribution of identity. Whatever name and identity the dream figure is given, he is always based on psychic elements of the dreaming mind.

REALITY AND MANIFESTATION

15 ∙– *The Man in the Moon*

"But what is more concrete than the I-Reality?" *Concrete.*

"Each of us can have direct experience of it at any moment." *Each of us.*

"Moreover the I-Reality is the only thing that is unquestionably known to us." *The only thing.* (The Maharshi, *Etudes*, p. 127)

He also tells us that the reality of objects is represented not by the form given them by craftsman or artist but by the material (gold or clay, for instance) of which they are made;

and that the principle of reality does not reside in the design of the painter but in the canvas on which it is painted, not in the apparently moving images of the cinema but in the surface on to which they are projected. Which is pure Vedanta and, I think, pure Zen.

Reality might, perhaps, be regarded as our texture, though not in a material sense but rather as conscious being, and its realisation as consciousness of being.

Could truth be more luminously suggested via our dualistic medium of words? Are these not fingers pointing directly at the Man in the Moon?

After all, our texture is Pure Consciousness, which is a definition of Reality Itself.

16 ⁃ You Must Dig Deep to Bury Your Shadow— A Causerie

We cannot dispose of our shadow by running away from it, nor can anyone bury his shadow, however deep the hole he may dig. A shadow can only be affected via the reality of which it is a distorted and unsubstantial projection.

The Maharshi is said to have pointed out that so it is with the ego. The I-concept can only be abandoned by seeking out the I-Reality of which it is a fluctuating and intangible reflection.

One may suspect that herein lies an essential divergence between the Vedantic and Zen-Taoist approach and that of modern Japanese Zen. The latter appears to seek satori by means of a manipulation of the psyche, a process that is represented by the Ko-an system of training, which seems to be in contradiction to the repeated affirmation of the T'ang

Masters that Mind cannot be reached through mind (or Reality through its shadow).

Dr. Hubert Benoit has revealed to us the mechanism of this process, whereby a diversion of the Attention to a conundrum, that has no significance in itself, isolates energy at its point of entry into manifestation, energy that would normally be disintegrated in futile affectivity and phantasy, and thereby promotes an accumulation without which the explosions of satori cannot readily take place. (*The Supreme Doctrine*, p. 103)

Quite so. But on what plane was the inventor of the Koan system operating? The Maharshi and Hsi Yun were speaking to us from the plane of Reality Itself.

Perhaps, however, we can use the shadow as an indication of the whereabouts of its source?

17 ·~ The Reason

Mentation being a dualistic activity implying both thinker and thought, "I" cannot reach the Witness of that activity Which is non-dual.

And the reason of *that* is that I *am* that impersonal Witness, and nothing else whatsoever.

ℭℭ

The third dimension is a concept and not a fact of perceptual experience, as we suppose. Which is presumably why animals are only aware of two at a time.

ℭℭ

The world around us is a concept, not a percept. It is a concept resulting from the percept of a percept ("ourselves") of the Unself.

❧

Our life is an elaborate analysis of a moment.

18 ·- Definitions - I

In an attempt to reduce confusion resulting from the use of manifold terms with diverse meanings by various authors, I propose henceforth to try the following neologisms:

THE DIVIDUAL—for individual, person, personality, self, me, "me's." We know that no such entity can exist as such, since the phenomenon is either to be described, physically, as a fluctuating force-field (an electronic flux in perpetual mutation), or, metaphysically, as an apparent objectivisation of consciousness, without permanence or any duration, renewed every instant and variable. Psychologically this phenomenon appears as a succession of "me's," multifarious and frequently contradictory, but this is merely an effect created by the identification of the I-concept with each impulse as it arises in the psyche.

THE IMPERSON—for the impersonal Witness, or relative self, Which, though Consciousness Itself, appears to observe both the thought and the supposed thinker thereof, and, as such, has to be indicated in dualistic language as an entity that at the same time is not such.

THE UNSELF—for the Self, pure Awareness, Consciousness, Reality, my Principle, Cosmic or Universal Mind,

Suchness, Quiddity, the Absolute, Godhead. The choice of this term to represent these hardly demands explanation.

This does not please anybody? Sorry. I will occasionally use the usual expressions so as not to deprive anybody of his right to incertitude.

19 ⸫ *The Great Joke*

The Imperson witnesses everything "we" do and everything "we" think (all psychic and physical manifestation), and that is the great joke. For we ourselves are the Imperson, and the "we" that acts and thinks is only a personalisation of the one Unself (Reality) seen as phenomenon, a notion that as phenomenon has neither permanence nor duration but is renewed every instant.

Duality (ignorance) is partial identification with the phenomenal "we," which has no real existence, due to the I-concept therein, and non-duality (wisdom) is the dissolution of that partial identification, leaving us in our normal and unalterable identification with the Unself.

The term "Imperson" is a dualistic term like any other, seeking to convey the essential impersonality of the Unself conceived, as is inevitable to us, as a "person" that is not such.

⸞⸟

It is difficult to approach more nearly by the use of words, which are essentially and incorrigibly dualist, but the Sages have sometimes made it clear that our best, perhaps our only, method of dissolving the false identification is by coming to recognise and to *know* ourselves as the witnessing Imperson, as which we both perceive "our" actions physical and mental (which are in no sense ours) and "ourselves" performing those actions (which in no sense do we perform).

20 ·~ Definitions of Non-attachment

"Non-attachment" in the sense of the Zen Masters, or as so translated from the Chinese, may sometimes mean awareness, but in the sense of non-attachment to all mental processes, i.e. thought and feeling, so that in the absence of "mentation" pure consciousness can flood in and take possession of the psyche.

That is a highly technical sense of what is ordinarily meant by Non-attachment or by Detachment, and that may be what the word Dhyana, so inadequately rendered by "Meditation," really implies.

The Zen Masters' condemnation of meditation applies to mental meditation, which implies thought, whereas Dhyana may imply non-mental (No-mind) meditation. Misunderstanding of the meaning of words, in translation, is the cause of much confusion.

21 ·~ Booing the Villain

It is as absurd to blame the historical personages for the parts they have played in history as it is to blame the personages of a novel or of a film.

It is no less absurd to blame our contemporaries in the moment of history in which ourselves are sustaining a role.

We may envy or pity those who have to play certain parts—that can hardly be called absurd, although ultimately we ourselves play every part and are the picture itself.

If to praise or to blame is evidently an example of failure to understand, is their extension, "loving" and "hating," any less idiotic?

Cock-a-doodle-do

The cock in Chantecler crows so proudly because he is convinced that it is his crowing that causes the sun to rise.

It would seem that Advaita Vedanta and the Lankavatara Sutra demonstrate that he is right and that it is indeed his crowing that causes the sun to rise. Did not that admirable philosopher Bishop Berkeley come to the same conclusion?

The Artichoke—Ecstasis

Every time our consciousness finds itself outside the range of domination by the I-concept, from whence the unreality of the ego, as of any concept, is apparent, a leaf is peeled off the artichoke.

The artichoke has many leaves, and the outer ones are coarser than the inner, but it becomes smaller at every mouthful. Finally nothing is left but the choke—and that is Reality.

22 ·- Integration

"There is no mind but Mind."

Nothing is permanent except Consciousness Itself. Everything, intelligence, sensation, the body, is discrete, without continuity or duration. Every momentary manifestation of every one of these notions is a fresh manifestation of

Consciousness Itself. That each such manifestation seems to resemble its immediate predecessor, giving the illusion of a continuous entity, has obscured the realisation of this essential condition.

This reveals the full meaning of what the Sages have told us, and we can see that Consciousness is the only Reality, alone IS, alone is us, and that there is nothing else to look for since It only is here and now.

It is us, we are It, anything else is just an apparent object of that Consciousness, i.e. a concept therein.

༅

At every moment and in all circumstances we must realise our identity with Consciousness Itself, once and for all we must see ourselves united Therewith, observe as the Witness Itself everything perceived via senses or mind, including that mind and body themselves, realising everything so observed as apparent objects within this Consciousness outside Which there can be nothing.

This is the transference of identification from the so-called psycho-somatic apparatus to Reality, but it is in fact merely the removal of a false identification and a return to the norm. Nothing any longer can be seen as from a subject, as the object of a subject that is other than pure and original Consciousness (Reality) Itself. I, we, no longer see, hear, touch, smell, taste, think, feel, for there is not, could not be, any I or we, which were only notions that transformed transitory objects of Consciousness into imaginary entities. Such imaginary entities were powerless to *do anything whatsoever*, they were only thoughts renewed every instant, apparent objectivisations of Consciousness Itself. "I," "we" *were* evaluations, notions, ideas: I, we *are* nothing but Consciousness,

Reality, and never could be anything else.

"We" have no percepts, concepts or ideas of any kind, "we" have nothing—for "*we*" do not exist, only Consciousness appears to have them, and as Consciousness we know them.

Now that we are seeing directly at last—have we understood what we ARE?

ॐ

That is the meaning of Vedanta Advaita, of the Lankavatara Sutra, of the Diamond Sutra, of Hui Neng, of Huang Po, of every explanation of the Maharshi.

Every authentic explanation coming from the plane of Reality tries to tell us just that. A re-statement, certainly not in any way "better" in itself, but in current language, may cause understanding to arise, but such understanding cannot come from the transient phenomenal aspect of mind: it can only come if an intuition of Consciousness Itself finds sudden dualistic expression via the projected mind.

23 ·– Débris – II

I do not experience: I am experience.

I am not the subject of *an* experience: I am that experience.

"I am" awareness. Nothing else can be I or can exist.

ॐ

An "event" may be inevitable, i.e. the product of circumstances, but our experience of that event is unconditioned—since there is nobody to experience the event apart from the experience itself.

❦

If time is reversed, and it needs must be reversible, what we describe as "effect" becomes "cause," and "cause" becomes "effect," for they are one. An event may be seen as the product of circumstances or circumstances may be seen as the product of an event. Experience of either is I. The electronic force-field in flux, through which experience occurs and which assumes an identity thereby, can only be what might be termed an externalisation of an aspect of the reality which we are.

The Eye

I am conscious but *I cannot be* conscious of Myself.
(In so far as ten words can express Truth. . . .)

❦

Phenomena only "exist" in the mind that perceives them.
(*Tibetan Book of the Dead,* 66)

❦

On the phenomenal plane we seek pleasure and the avoidance of pain. On the noumenal plane we know the absence of both—which is bliss.

❦

What may be meant by "reincarnation"? That the dream goes on, for death is merely a phenomenon and changes nothing but appearances.

24 ·~ Pure Consciousness

Only as Pure Consciousness am I conscious of anything.

Only Pure Consciousness is conscious of anything, for only as Pure Consciousness am I myself conscious.

Therefore only as Pure Consciousness does anything exist. There is no other consciousness, no other "mind."

Everything that seems other than Pure Consciousness, i.e. every "object" of consciousness—myself, you, thought or object "perceived," is a notion in Pure Consciousness. But why does Pure Consciousness have notions?

Tao

What is the use of talking about the objects of consciousness, whether they be thoughts, sensations or hot-water bottles? Objects must have a subject, subject-object is a pair of opposites, like all others, which are two halves of one whole. That whole is whatever you choose to call it. But as Reality has Unreality as its other half, Being—Non-Being, Absolute—Relative, and so on *ad infinitum* (even "non-dual Consciousness" is opposed by "Dual Consciousness," "Pure Consciousness" by "Impure," "Universal Mind" by "Particular"), either a term that has no apparent meaning, that is unconditioned, such as "Tao" must be used and on the understanding that it must necessarily be identical with "Non-Tao"—whatever that could be, or else both pairs of opposites must be used together. And why not? Does not such a composite term help us to *realise* what it implies? "Reality-Unreality," "Consciousness-Unconsciousness," "Absolute-Relative," "Universal-Particular Mind," "Duality-Non-Duality," "Dual—Non-dual Consciousness." In other words—Tao.

There can be no objects of consciousness anyhow: there can only be subject-objects which are Consciousness-Unconsciousness Itself. Everything is just—Tao.

❦

Mind versus Matter is unreal, like all dualism, but Mind-Matter as a suchness is real. To realise the latter is at least as important as it is to realise the former. Usually, however, the former alone is pointed out—and the unfortunate pilgrim is left with the impression that both are unreal, whereas, in fact, each is unreal but *both* are real.

Each half of every pair of opposites is unreal. Both halves of every pair of opposites, united in their quiddity, are Reality-Unreality, or Tao.

The reunion of every pair of opposites renders them non-dual.

That is approximately as far as words can carry one towards understanding the nature of—Tao.

❦

L'Inconcevable—give it any other name or label you wish . . .for it can never be other than that.

TIME AND SPACE

25 ·- *Transcending Space*

Man has never had any difficulty in stopping time, mentally, but he sees it as immobile space. His highest flight is to compensate the negation of time by extending Space—as in the

Linga-sharira, or Long-body, all we are from birth to death stretched out like a snake.

Can we be satisfied with this? But in order to negate Space we can only extend or contract it. And whichever we do, if we do it wholeheartedly, what we arrive at is a void. The Void? What more do we want? Did not the Lord Buddha tell us that was all there was anyway?

∞

Space is only the distance between objects, i.e. a concept, an idea, a notion.

Dualism Is a Function of Tridimensionality

The relativity of the universe as perceived by us is a consequence of the limitation in our perception of dimensions. When that sensorial limitation in directions of measurement is removed, the separation of subject and object ceases and we unite with the ten thousand things in unicity.

26 ∽ Transcending Time

The Linga Sharira, or Long Body, refers to the total or composite body of a man from birth to death as it should be revealed if the time-process in which it is perceived consecutively were to be transcended.

But are we not also the totality of our forebears and descendants, or, in a spatial but non-temporal image, one element of that—to us—vast total body? We must all be one "body"— from the "beginning" to the "end" as perceived in the time concept, one vast body of which each (to us) individual may be likened to a cell.

However, to transcend the temporal concept while retaining the spatial seems to have little sense, save that it is easier to conceive. Our notion of timelessness is just immobility, what we describe as "time standing still." But spacelessness is harder on the mind. To deprive the vast body, which the removal of time has left on our hands, of its spatial character, is to reduce it to nullity or void, for even the tiniest point we can imagine occupies space.

"Body" implies "matter," and matter implies extension in space. To follow this concept leads us beyond the boundaries of our mind and into the region of unicity in which we really are.

REALITY AND MANIFESTATION

27 ·– *The Dreamer*

I

ONE: The universe is My dream. Every thing therein, including "you" and "me," is an element of that dream—from elephant to virus, from nebula to atom.

TWO: Then each of us dreams a universe? How comes it that we all dream the same universe?

ONE: Each of us does not dream *a* universe. Only I dream *the* universe. You all perceive the same universe because you are all elements in My dream.

TWO: Is that concept not—let us say—somewhat egotistic?

ONE: "Egoism" is a dualistic concept and implies "non-egoism." But there is no such thing in reality as non-egoism. Therefore there is no egoism either. There is

27

only I—and nothing else (which would be necessary) to constitute egoism.

TWO: But why is the universe your dream any more than mine?

ONE: I have already told you: "you" do not exist except as dreamed by Me.

TWO: Supposing I reply that "you" do not exist except as dreamed by *Me?*

ONE: That is unnecessary: it goes without saying.

TWO: There is evidently something I have failed to understand.

ONE: That is due to our dualistic language, inadequate to the communication of truth. We have to use the same word to convey several meanings. You are still thinking in terms of identification with a body. You are using the terms "you" and "me" in order to indicate the unreal elements of My dream which are holding this conversation. Unreal elements of a dream cannot dream the universe of which they are elements.

TWO: Then who dreams it?

ONE: I do. Anyone who says "I do." For that I is the Absolute, Reality, Consciousness Itself, Cosmic Mind, Tao. That I is One—no matter who says it.

TWO: Obscure, very obscure!

ONE: "Obscure" my foot! It is as clear as daylight, as simple and obvious as anything within the grasp of Mind in manifestation. Only its expression is obscure—for it has been expressed in words.

TWO: So I am everything in this universe, as I am everything in the universe of my sleeping dreams, every elephant, every virus, every nebula, every atom, "you" and "I"?

ONE: You have understood.

TWO: What more is there to say?

ONE: Nothing whatsoever. Everything is explained, every word of every Sage and Master. That is the meaning of the Lord Buddha expressly conveyed in the Lankavatara Sutra, and Sri Krishna if he be regarded as responsible for Vedanta Advaita.

II

TWO: Let me quote the Lanka: "The world which is mind-manifested is stirred up by the wind of objectivity, it evolves and dissolves," i.e. it is of us and we are of it.

ONE: ". . . recognition of the truth that an external world is nothing but the Mind itself" (LVIII).

TWO: "As they tenaciously cling to the thought of an ego-soul and all that belongs to it, they are really unable to understand what is meant by the doctrine of Mind-only" (LXXI). That was precisely my case five minutes ago!

ONE: "And when he thus recognises *the non-existence of the external world, which is no more than his own mind,* he is said to have the will-body" (LVII). Nothing exists outside the Mind.

TWO: These elements of My dream, which seem to dream a universe, in their turn, when asleep—that is, "you" and "me"—we are quite unreal?

ONE: Words again. Nothing is quite unreal, not even a mirage, a reflection, an echo: all are manifestations of Mind. But none is an entity.

TWO: You have said that Non-reality does not exist.

ONE: How could it? It is one part of a dualistic concept.

TWO: Then Reality does not exist?

ONE: How could it? It is one part of a dualistic concept.

TWO: Then what exists?

ONE: Reality-Non-Reality, conveniently suggested by a term such as Tao!

TWO: Can one go any further?

ONE: Yes, it is the gateway. But words cannot take us through the gate.

III

TWO: The Lanka you have just quoted says that he who thus recognises that the external world is only his own mind is said to have the will-body. What is that?

ONE: *Manomayakaya,* mind-made body, no doubt the "body" of the mind attained by a bodhisattva, freed from "birth-and-death."

TWO: These Sanscrit terms and the concepts they imply are difficult for us to grasp.

ONE: It is not necessary for us to grasp them, nor always helpful. Professor Suzuki's comment is enough: "The Lankavatara will still insist on the doctrine of 'Mind-only,' saying that it is a fact of immediate perception and that enlightenment or spiritual freedom comes upon one after realising this fact within oneself." Is that not clear?

TWO: Perfectly. But has "will-body" any corresponding sense in terms of Western thought?

ONE: Might it not be the "self"-consciousness Ouspensky and Gourdjieff sought to develop from what they termed "the essence" by a complex system of training, working from without inwards, and which alone, according to those doctrines, enables man to avoid extinction or eternal recurrence in time?

TIME AND SPACE

28 ·~ *Uncommon-Sense Regarding Reincarnation*

If, in some manner not hitherto revealed to us, reincarnation, as popularly conceived and so very *tacitly* accepted by eminent Buddhists, should in fact be possible, and since Time is a factor personal to each of us, it must necessarily also be normal, and as usual, for us to reincarnate into the Past and to have reincarnated into the Future.

No doubt we *have* often visited the moon in a space-ship, and we *shall be* Julius Caesar and Cleopatra—and some of Louis XIV's kitchen-staff?

But we still ask the Masters, so taciturn on this delicate subject, what it is that reincarnates—since the Enlightened One Himself never tired of telling us that there is not anything in the way of an ego-entity, a personality, a being, or a separated individuality.

The transcendental, unconditioned I-Reality, which escapes this thorough-going definition can hardly be concerned in a process subject to Time. Therefore it can only be conditioned, relative, hypothetical elements that carry on this traffic in their own times. After all, they are our "me"s, and Past and Future exist in a dimension that surrounds us and that may be accessible.

Perhaps each of us is distributed among Julius Caesar, Cleopatra, Louis XIV's kitchen staff, moon-tourists, etc., all at the, and in the, same Time?

PHYSICS AND METAPHYSICS

29 ·- *Unicity - I*

When you give a shilling to a beggar—do you realise that you are giving it to yourself?

When you help a lame dog over a stile—do you realise that you yourself are being helped?

When you kick a man when he is down—do you realise that you are kicking yourself?

Give him another kick—if you deserve it!

Unicity - II

Surely revenge—*tu quoque,* tit-for-tat, an eye for an eye, the normal, eternal, fatuous, universal human reaction, automatic in the young and the primary, is just a function of split unity?

Hit him back: you hit yourself because you hit yourself previously in the time sequence. Only if you divide one into two halves can such things happen.

One good turn . . . tic-toc—a symbolic reconstruction of unity split by time into a sequence, symbolic because such a reconstruction cannot effectually occur in time. We call it balance, compensation, even harmony. Is it not a reflex attempt to reintegrate the state of unicity in which intemporally we are?

REALITY AND MANIFESTATION

30 ·~ Good Morning

ONE: Good Morning. How are you?

THE OTHER: I am. And you?

ONE: As cross as two sticks.

THE OTHER: Who is cross? And how can there be *two* sticks?
          Is one not enough?

ONE: Who is cross? I am, of course.

THE OTHER: Impossible. Of what are you speaking?

ONE: My ego.

THE OTHER: Your *what?*

ONE: My ego.

THE OTHER: Whatever is that?

ONE: The ego, e-g-o, the confounded thing that keeps us
         all imprisoned, the identification No. 1, the cause of
         all the trouble.

THE OTHER: I know of no such thing. Does it exist, and if
          so—where? I have never seen anything of the kind.
          You are suffering from hallucinations. You shouldn't
          let yourself imagine things.

ONE: Hang it all, we all have an ego. It may be an illusion
         and all that, in fact we know that it is, but, living as
         we do, we are cross and offended and this and that,
         and what is it that feels all that sort of thing but
         our ego?

THE OTHER: You are as firmly tied up in your dualistic ver-
          biage as a kitten in a ball of wool.

ONE: Well, then, unwind me, like a good fellow.

THE OTHER: That would be a laborious process; let's cut the
          wool. The ego is a concept, as you well know, a
          notion, at the very most a working hypothesis, a

supposition, an algebraic symbol like *pi,* something posited in order to serve as a basis for the explanation of the inexplicable.

ONE: Quite unreal and all that. Yes, yes, well do we know it!

THE OTHER: Well do you know it—and yet you go on behaving exactly as though you still believed it to be reality. You go on attributing your reactions to something you say you know to be imaginary. And you go on being indignant with other people for being subject to a thing you know to be imaginary. In short you know it to be only a notion, a concept, and yet you continue to think of it as real.

ONE: But if I am cross, and I am, what is it that is feeling like that if it is not my ego that is still there is spite of my knowledge that it is not?

THE OTHER: Face facts, face facts! If it is not there—how can it be cross? Or offended? Or anything else imaginable?

ONE: But I am cross, furious.

THE OTHER: Nonsense. You are not anything. That is only an act you are putting on. You are playing a part—and attributing your reactions to an imaginary ego. Crossness, or any other emotional reaction, is only colouring-matter you add to affectivity. You are blowing bubbles and giving them names and attributes. When they burst you will know them for what they are—just passing deflections of reality in your mind.

ONE: Although I know the ego is not a reality, I am still behaving as though it were. Still assuming it, still thinking of it, still attributing my reactions to it. Yes, yes, I am. But do not we all? What does it add up to?

THE OTHER: The number you first thought of; zero.

34

Intellectual understanding without assimilation is the frame without the picture.

ONE: How does one insert a picture?

THE OTHER: I said *the* picture. The canvas is now covered by your highly-coloured emotional imaginings. Perfection is attained, as St. Exupéry pointed out, not when there is nothing more to add, but when there is nothing more to discard.

ONE: We should suppress our emotional reactions?

THE OTHER: If you could, it would only produce the effect known as psychic traumatism.

ONE: So what?

THE OTHER: We are now discussing the elementary confusion between mental vacancy and the void that is plenitude. Correct attention, supra-sensual affectivity, are uncoloured by emotional reactions. That is the picture which is no picture, within the frame that is no longer a frame.

ONE: Can any ordinary chap do that?

THE OTHER: Why not? There is nothing to do. It is there already, always, the only permanent and immutable aspect of what you are.

ONE: But how does one get at it?

THE OTHER: You say that you are cross. As the Maharshi told you to do—ask yourself, *who* is cross? And what is "cross" anyhow? You will see at once that there is nothing anywhere that could be cross, and no such thing as crossness. Bubbles calling one another names! Prick them. Bang, (imaginary bang of imaginary bubbles), they have vanished! What is left?

ONE: Correct attention, supra-sensual affectivity, pure as light, transparent as light, just—awareness!

THE OTHER: At last you have understood! Let us start

afresh:—Good Morning. How are you?
ONE: I am. And you?
THE OTHER: As cross as one stick!

TIME AND SPACE

31 ·- The House of Cards

I

Ouspensky demonstrated that an angle in any direction of
measurement beyond those that are accessible to living creatures is inevitably interpreted as Movement. It follows from
this that movement is the interpretation of a spatial concept.

But Time is the measure of movement; that is its function,
and to that end we imagined it. It has acquired the status of
a fundamental principle—but it is only the measurement of
the interpretation of an idea.

From the idea of Time, of duration, springs Memory,
which consists of images of what the senses have perceived,
ranged in series like books on a shelf, as a direct result of this
notion of Time according to which we see in succession its
interpretation of a spatial concept.

From Memory springs the notion of a self, a notion which
depends on memories, and which also depends on Time, on
duration, in order that it may be conceived. Accordingly the
self is a notion which depends on a notion which itself is the
interpretation of an idea.

The whole of this "house of cards" is an imaginary structure, a tower of notions, ideas, concepts, that is, of thoughts.
Its only reality lies in the fact that the sensation of an "I" is,
derived in this manner, the I-Reality, the "I am," interpreted
under the influence of the idea of succession—which is

Time. If we follow it, trace it back through its derivations to its origin, we find ourselves in our own origin, in Reality.

Just as the Maharshi told us, again and again, to do in all circumstances.

Note: The concept of an angle in a further dimension, seen as movement, may seem difficult but only demands consideration. A dog in a motor-car is believed to see trees and houses, habitually stationary in his experience, turning as he approaches and passes them. Hence his peculiar excitement and delight.

But someone may say "Even so, why an angle?" Look about you; what do you see? *Circles?*

II

Is it not comforting to think that our dear self—and how dear!—is our reality after all, regarded serially, in succession, by temporal vision which so conceives all movement which, itself, is only an interpretation of the immutable seen as an angle! But, alas, it is only a question of the I-concept. That which people call the "self," the "ego," etc., is an aggregation of emotional forces, passions, desires, avidities, etc., all dualistic, which attach themselves to the personal notion and which thereby appear to form an entity, or even several entities—the "me's," as some people prefer to call them. But there can be such entity, or entities; these affective concepts are dualistic, each one half of a pair of opposites, or complementaries, each a scissor, and thereby entirely deprived of reality. This aggregation around the personal concept does not constitute anything whatsoever; it is just composed of thoughts without substance, vapours dissolving in the air.

Let us not forget, either, that the "self," the "ego," so conceived, being illusory—a thought, based on a thought, which is based on a thought, itself based on a thought, there cannot be such a thing as our sacrosanct Free-will, no, not the slightest trace of it, as far as our actions are concerned, in view of the fact that there is no "self" to exercise it! That is the pill that sticks in the throat of nearly everybody. Nevertheless, once swallowed it stays down. What a comic notion, after all, that a perfectly illusory self, which is only an idea, could be possessed of a will and know how to direct its destiny in the face of and against everybody by means of another imaginary concept known by the name of "free-will"! And all the others, with their imaginary "selves," each with his imaginary "free-will"? What a traffic-jam! The so-called "will" itself is only, as most of us are aware, the emotive impulsion of desire.

Overboard with these absurdities! Let us grow up even if we cannot wake up! We have seen that those who are awake, the sages who have spoken to us from that condition, knew what they were talking about, spoke the truth, and told us what they knew and all they could, particularly in trying to get us to understand that none of these notions exist.

Reality alone exists—and that we are. All the rest is only a dream, a dream of the One Mind, which is our mind without the "our." Is it so hard to accept? Is it so difficult to assimilate and to *live?*

REALITY AND MANIFESTATION

32 ·- Dreams and Reality

Without losing your belief in the existence of a self you will be as far from losing your belief that you are unawakened as you were when you first heard of the Buddha.

෨

It is not sufficient to understand that everything about us, including ourselves, is a dream structure. The Masters make it clear that we must go further and understand the ultimate reality of phenomena, i.e. that all dream structures are a manifestation of Mind, of Mind which is ourselves.

Surely that is the meaning of the well-known saying about the mountains and rivers ceasing to appear as such to the pilgrim on the way, but once more becoming mountains and rivers when he comes to the end of the path?

෨

Real seeing requires no eyes—for there is no one to see.

TIME AND SPACE

33 ·- Free-will - III

One observes, perhaps with compassion, the rather pitiful attempts of all but the very wise to seize any loop-hole for what they call free-will. Always you find the Note, or the parenthesis, giving hope. They are like drowning men clutching at any objects that remain afloat. They just cannot reconcile themselves to the abandonment of the notion that an imaginary entity can do whatever it wants whenever it wishes, and without reference to the Mind that imagined it.

The idea seems like suicide to them. But even if you do feel like that about it—which means that you have not understood—why cling to a last pitiful remnant of illusion as though it could save you from anything but enjoying clear vision at last! And if it *is* suicide—is not that just what you seek—the extinction of your "self," the "death" of the "old" man?

Enfin: Can anyone who talks about free-will have understood? Is it not a hallmark of non-comprehension?

Note: As Reality you are free, of course, but your "will" is that of the Cosmos.

REALITY AND MANIFESTATION

34 ·- *La Vida Es Sueño*

The apparent self in our dreams believes in himself; the sea or motor-car in front of him is real, dangerous, powerful or whatever it may be, and the people, some of them to us long dead, are as real as they were when we knew them. The mind that dreams our dreams dreams as convincingly as the mind that dreams our so-called waking life. When we awaken, our critical mind, applying its waking standards, sees the dream personages as unreal, as distorted, as fantastic, as what it calls "figments of the imagination."

And those who awaken from their "waking" dream, from the dream of "daily life," can we doubt that they see their "waking" dream personages as we see those of our sleeping dreams, i.e. as unreal, distorted, fantastic, as figments of the imagination? From their words it seems clear that they do, and that so it is.

Neither dream, and there are other kinds of dream experienced in other states, to which the same applies, is one whit more or less real than the other, for both, all, are mind-manifestations experienced by consciousness in different conditions.

The only reality in either, in any kind of dream, of mind-manifestation, is Mind Itself.

BRIEF CAUSERIES

35 ⌐ The One Freedom

I was free from the idea of an ego-entity, a personality,
a being, and a separated individuality.
—THE BUDDHA in the Diamond Sutra, XIV

All Western life is based on the reality of an ego. Commerce, culture, science and religion have this reality of the individual entity as a basic principle, which itself is an element of the belief that phenomena are real and that noumenon is unreal. In the East, so we are told, this is not so, at least has not been so hitherto and is not so yet to any serious extent, for the oriental religions, in their purer manifestations, Vedanta as Advaita and Buddhism uncorrupted, have inculcated the contrary since before our civilisations were born.

Increasingly in the West we are coming to understand that the oriental understanding is correct, and that Noumenon alone is real. This understanding once existed in our civilisation, for the Greek sages knew it, and it is implicit in Gnostic Christianity.

We need not be surprised, therefore, nor disheartened, by the apparent inability of the Western mind to overcome its inhibition, which is the probable explanation of the rarity or absence of enlightenment among us, for the Western intellect comprehends the truth readily enough, but resistance to the total assimilation of that truth is too great. The company of those who comprehend intellectually is still a small one, though it may be rising from a few hundreds to a few thousands in each country, but the percentage or per mil-age of those who have really understood seems to remain at zero. Do we, in fact, know anybody, famous or obscure, who in thought, in speech, and in writing does not refer to "*the* ego," "*the* self," *as though* such an entity really existed? That seems to be conclusive evidence, betraying the state of mind that has not understood. The Buddha and the Sages, when they found it necessary to refer to the concept, used—in translation at least—the indefinite article, "a" self, thereby implying that they spoke of a notion and not of a real entity.

Intellectual comprehension that no such entity could exist is insufficient. It does not in fact even loosen the stranglehold of the concept, and an "act of faith" does not affect it either. On the contrary, each time the existence of the notion as an entity is referred to as a "fact," even tacitly assumed, its imaginary power is thereby affirmed and the possibility of liberation—for liberation is liberation from that—is rendered more remote.

Why should this be so? I think that can be explained in simple words. A non-existent entity cannot be supposed to be capable of experiencing *anything real*—and reality is presumably just that! Such a proceeding would imply the dualistic perception of reality as an object by another object which itself is unreal.

The I is real, as long as it remains unconditioned. It exists in its own state because it IS its own state of enlightenment, bliss, satori. No experience is called-for, no experience can be had, there is nothing to be attained. If the illusion, the concept that *We* are phenomena can be dissipated, we are just real, that which we are, all that we are; and that is the so-called "state" of enlightenment, of being "awake."

The Lord Buddha said it, the Lord Krishna said it, it

seems evident that the Lord Jesus knew it, and among the awakened Masters, Hui Neng said it, Huang Po said it, Padma Sambhava said it, the Maharshi said it—and, all things considered, relatively little else. Is there much else to say? How slim are the books devoted to the ultimate words of the Awakened—the *Diamond Sutra*, the *Wei Lang Sutra*,* the *Baghavad Gita*, even the *Upanishads*, the *Seeing of Reality*, *Who am I?!*** And if the superfluous, which even these books have managed to acquire, were eliminated, including oriental repetition, only a few pages would remain to each. That is all we need. That should be enough. But we should need to persuade ourselves once and for all and at last—that they meant what they said and, once and for all and at last—to believe them!

PHYSICS AND METAPHYSICS

36 ·- Unicity - III

The further direction of measurement inevitably interpenetrates our tridimensional universe. That further direction of measurement is imperceptible to our sensorial apparatus, but our minds (plural purely conventional), being imperceptible, presumably function along that dimension.

---

* *Ed. note:* i.e. the *Hui Neng Sutra; Wei Lang* is the same name rendered in the Southern dialect of T'ang Dynasty Chinese.

** WWW is here referring to the replies given by Sri Ramana Maharshi to certain questions posed by Sivaprakasam Pillai, subsequently compiled and published under the title *Who Am I?*

Apparently confined by our three directions of measurement, we think we only communicate along those three, so we shout at one another, kick or kiss one another, look at one another with or without magnifying glasses. Our contacts are exclusively superficial, and we judge one another, react to one another by liking and disliking, in a crude manner based on this contact that is confined to our three superficial dimensions only of approach. Never by this method can we know more than the surface of one another, or of anything, for never can we make contact otherwise than by a surface touching a surface.

Meanwhile our minds, functioning in a further direction of measurement which cannot but interpenetrate the three that our senses enable us to know, are in permanent contact inevitably unfettered by our temporal and spatial limitations of interpretation.

Our *minds*, which are mind itself interpreted as "us," are ultimately one, but in so far as differentiation emanating from "us" segregates them "around" us they fulfill the function of communication by the mere impulsion of desire on our part for such communication, and without the application of any cumbrous technique such as our dualistic system of words.

How strange that we do not seem to know this! Not knowing it, we do not consciously use it. Yet it certainly takes place "behind our backs." Why do we not use it? Some of us do without knowing it; others use it deliberately. Does it require an elaborate technique? My guess is that it is just about as difficult as riding a bicycle. But it surely cannot be used except by those who know, understand, realise that it is there to be used.

Having realised that much, it is barely a step to the realisation that just a little further from the periphery—our minds are all one and the same mind, and that there is nothing else.

"To one who has discovered his real nature, how can there be anywhere or anything separate from it?" (Huang Po, *Wan Ling Record,* 43)

TIME AND SPACE

37 · The Bogie

We talk a great deal about dualism, lecture one another about it, and fill the pages of our books—usually about its misdeeds. Yet I do not remember any one of us mentioning the detail of what it is. One might almost suspect that we do not know.

May one venture in where even bodhisattvas seem to fear to tread? Tentatively, of course, not like bulls in Chinese philosophy-shops.

Conceptual thought—that is, human thought, thought as differentiated from pure perception—is essentially linguistic and inseparable from expression in words. (Animal language is non-verbal and non-dualistic.) Conceptual, linguistic thought is incapable of seizing and expressing the Absolute, Unicity, the Thusness of anything. Its dimensional limitations oblige it to differentiate. In so doing it forms a dualism, it sees something as "good" relatively to another thing as "bad" in order to form a concept at all of the Thusness it is seeking to conceive. One half has to be compared to the other half in order that anything can be expressed.

Dualism, therefore, seems only to be a trick of thought, not a real thing in any sense, itself a notion, a concept, a description of the process to which thought has to be subjected. Therefore, in order to transcend it, thought itself has to be transcended.

That is why the Awakened insist—and *how* they insist—that the suspension or transcendence of conceptual thinking is the *sine qua non* of realisation.

Having achieved the power of conceptual thought, man is called upon to go beyond it.

❧

This dimensional limitation may be attributed to the concept of Time, to which we are subject, for no two thoughts can occur simultaneously. We have to conceive anything as something in our memorial vocabulary, and then in comparison with something else, and relativity is born—yet another notion or concept. If we could short-circuit Time and think both thoughts at once the relativity and the dualism would thereby disappear. So dualism is seen as a result of the limiting dimension of Time.

❧

It may be that dualism applies also to perception and so the dualistic process is responsible for manifestation, manifestation being the product of polarity, for all manifestation seems to result from the interplay of the factors Yang and Yin.

Duality seems to be inherent in our perception of nature. The duplication of organs in all forms of life is a remarkable feature of the world as we know it, and we ourselves are composed of two relative concepts that are betrayed in our physical as in our psychic appearance. If you take the trouble to duplicate each half of a full-face photograph of any fully-grown human being (by printing one half of the film back-to-front, thus making a full-face of each half) you will always find yourself looking at two photographs, one of which, for differentiation's sake, may be called that of a bodhisattva, and the other that of a gangster. Perhaps you would rather I termed them the Yin-personality and the Yang-personality?

It seems unlikely that even the Awakened transcend this duality of perception, for the perceptions even of the Awakened are presumably still subject to Time. It is probably enough that we transcend conceptual dualism in order to open our eyes in Reality, that we wake up from our own mental dream as such, remaining in the dream of the One Mind as long as we wear our flesh and use its organs.

Note: The concept-making mind is an inhibitory instrument.

38 ⸱ The Three Known Dimensions are External: The Fourth Is Within the Mind

Since there are no "things" we nevertheless conceive of three directions of measurement in order to measure our mind-created projections, but further directions of measurement can only be conceived as within the mind itself.

Dimensions do not lie in a mind-made Universe, but in the aspect of mind that seeks to interpret it.

So-called spiritual experience is the development of a further dimension in the mind. By the cultivation of intuition this new direction of measurement is explored.

The Sages, the Masters, are men who are able to use a further dimension of mind which is present in all of us.

Free-will - IV

Mind in so far as it is unconditioned is "free," i.e. in so far as it is Mind and not *our* mind, the unconditioned aspect of our mind being Mind, and the conditioned aspect of Mind being "our" mind.

"Owing to worldly beliefs, which *he is free to accept or reject,* man wanders in the Sangsara." (Padma Sambhava)

39 ·– *The Present Includes Past and Future*

We tend to think of Past, Present and Future as events external to ourselves which we see, suffer, experience by force of circumstances. But Past, Present and Future are nothing of the sort! They are notions of our own which we apply to our experiences of life.

We have a little search-light in our minds, and that which it lights up is what we think is the Present. It seems to be mounted on a mechanical appliance which moves in inaudible jerks every fraction of a second. What it has illumined we call the Past, what it will, or may, illumine we call the Future. There is no reason to attribute movement to that which is lit up: movement is an illusion inherent in the source. It is surprisingly like the projection of a cinematographic film during which the only movement is that of the film itself, both light and screen being immobile. In both cases the Present, the individual "still," is never perceived, and the sequence of these produces the illusion of motion. Our attention is the motive-power of the Time-apparatus.

Science too, science particularly, has been deceived into assuming the external reality of what is perceived, whereas we know now, and can see, that the apparently external is a mind-projection of our own apparatus.

"The past has not gone. The present is a fleeting moment. The future is not yet-to-come." (Huang Po, *The Wan Ling Record,* 55)

REALITY AND MANIFESTATION

40 ·– *The Communication of Knowledge and the Communication of Understanding*

Why did the Masters rarely preach, which we unhappily term lecture nowadays? Indeed did they ever—in the sense of our word lecture?

The words of the Buddha are usually in reply to a question posed by Subhuti, Mahatma or another, whose function that seems to be. The words of Krishna are in the form of a dialogue with Arjuna. We are authoritatively told that the character, strange to some of us, of the *Upanishads,* is due to this fact. "*C'est ne pas comprende le point essentiel: l'enseignement spirituel indien est toujours une réponse à une question particulière, le dialogue entre le maître et son disciple ne s'achevant que lorsque tous deux participent à la même conscience, à la même vision des choses.*"

The words of Huang Po are replies to questions put by P'ei Hsin and others.

The *Seeing of Reality* of Padma Sambhava seems to be a kind of testament on the part of a dying man in reply to a general question put by the disciples surrounding his death-bed.

Nearly every word we have of the Maharshi is in reply to a question.

I think we can say that the great, the real masters, the

Awakened, did not preach, or lecture, and that their rare utterances that are not technically replies to specific questions are nevertheless in fact replies to questions that are present in the minds of their audience.

The reason for this is not far to seek. Understanding, other than purely intellectual, demands a participation other than purely intellectual apprehension, and without such participation the discourse would be wasted, if not harmful.

But are not our lectures just this last?

Perhaps the Masters did not desire to teach, but only to enlighten?

41 ·~ The Spanner

The I-concept is not a necessary evil; it is necessary but it is not an evil.

Every living thing must have the sensation of itself, just as every "thing," animate or inanimate, from nebula to atom, must have a centre, without which it would disintegrate. This has been pointed out.

The spanner in the works is not the I-concept which, unconditioned, is REAL, but the aggregation of affective impulses which gather round it and form a purely imaginary entity, built up from memories, which appears as an impersonation.

That is the inexistent thing, the notion that must be subjected to dis-aggregation, which must be pulled to pieces, resolved into its vaporous component elements and reduced to a state of dissolution. Notions, however aggregated, do not constitute a thing or an entity. Zeros (nothing), added or multiplied, never become anything but zero. A structure composed of a million notions could never be anything but a notion itself, and the only reality it could ever have would be the I-reality whose conditioned aspect, the I-concept, allowed the dream notions to *appear.*

Note: It might be objected that in seeming to attribute to animals, insects, reptiles, birds, and even inanimate objects, an I-concept I am exceeding my commission, since the concept as such cannot exist in their aspect of Mind.

In the case of non-human creatures the term might rather be "I-percept," though the personal sense may be entirely unconscious. Since all creatures and objects are themselves just concepts it is only a question of the degree of evolution of the notion of self which is to be attributed to them.

PHYSICS AND METAPHYSICS

42 · The Column of Smoke

We all know that the idea of a phenomenal self is altogether dependent on memory. From memories the notion has been built up, as a house is constructed of bricks.

Memory is a series of records—photographs if you will—of sense perceptions of past presents. Therefore it is subject to Time. Without Time there could be no memory, outside Time the notion of memory makes nonsense for there could be nothing to remember (since one cannot remember an absolute present).

The unreality of Time was realised by several of the Greek philosophers, and, in our civilisation, by Immanuel Kant, who recognised it as a fabrication of our receptive apparatus. Modern science has arrived at this conception and has linked it with Space. The Enlightened, of all races and ages, could not fail to know this, and it is implicit, where it is not explicit, in their teaching.

Time is basically a spatial concept, and is essentially the measure of movement. Ouspensky saw it as our interpretation of the limiting dimension. We, or quadrupeds, reptiles or birds, can only see the superior dimension, that which lies beyond those to which our senses are attuned, in series, as one thing after another, and so in movement which, in the sense in which we use the term habitually it measures, or can be used to measure by means of mechanical appliances. It is, therefore, ultimately a measure of Space-interpreted-as-movement.

Analysing the matter still more closely, the notion of Movement may be an interpretation—erroneous in a sense, and so a misinterpretation—of angles in the superior dimension, and what the senses perceive, or appear to perceive in our mind-made universe, is dependent on angles—straight lines and circles being theoretical only. If we care to imagine a duodimensional being encountering an angle, such angle necessarily being in the third (superior) dimension, he would presumably be dumbfounded, and as he approached it the object would appear to move (though it would be himself who was in fact in movement).

Starting from the notion of a self or ego we have reached the origin of this concept, tracing it from notion to notion, each notion derived from another, through five degrees of interpretation until we arrived at a direction of measurement of Space inaccessible to our sense-perceptions and interpreted as Movement of which Time is the measure. But Space itself is a notion, and a direction of measurement is only a geometrical conception. It is a column of smoke in which the only reality is the "I" which poses the question.

43 ⁓ *Other Aspects of the Dream We Are Living*

We observe the solar systems, and the atomic systems, as worlds or specks of matter connected internally, and to us, by forces to which we have given names such as gravity, attraction-and-repulsion, magnetic fields, but the fact simply is that the limitation of our senses only enables us to perceive the "worlds" and "specks" as what we call matter, and the links between them as invisible forces known to us by inference or through instruments more sensitive than ourselves. If our senses were other than they are we might perceive the linking forces as solid whereas the material objects themselves might be invisible.

We can scarcely doubt that neither matter nor forces of attraction-and-repulsion are in themselves more or less "solid" or "imponderable" the one than the others, for such are merely evaluations, and that with still more adequate sensorial apparatus we should perceive the whole cosmic set-up as one homogenous and continuous structure.

℘

In front of me, where I have luncheon, there are geraniums growing. From day to day I see bright-red flowers budding, flowering, fading, and being replaced by others. Radionic apparatus—to the surprise of its operators—has photographed a flower in full bloom when only a seed was placed before its lens. So the flower was already there; the flower was there *too!*

When the Maharshi was on his death-bed he asked what people were weeping about. When he was informed he commented: "But where do they imagine I could go to?"

May we not be geraniums? We ourselves only perceive the

53

flowers when they come into manifestation, when their rate of vibration, shall we say, brings them within the scope of perception of our sensorial apparatus, and when they fade out of it (to where?) we say that they are "dead," and watch them being replaced by others which, in their turn, vibrate into manifestation (from where?), i.e. to within the scope of perception of our sensorial apparatus.

Do they know that they all spring from one seed, that they all existed in that seed, that they only exist as "geraniums in flower" in so far as we are able to see them as such for a given period and while they maintain a given rate in their scale of vibration?

❧

Jack and Jill, Georges et Marie are sitting round a table, with Jumbo beside them, hoping for a biscuit, and Minouche asleep in an armchair nearby. No doubt they think of themselves as totally isolated individuals (the four who are cursed with thought), communicating noisily by means of a system nearly as cumbersome as the system of flags which ships used to use to communicate at sea.

But are they? If our senses, the senses of you and me who are looking through the window, were more adequate than they are, might we not see all six "material" objects and the magnetic fields surrounding them, with the attractions-and-repulsions connecting them, as one continuous whole? Or might we not perceive the attractions and repulsions as visible, and the "material" objects as merely inferential, so that the communications between them were real and continual and immediate, and their clamorous interchange of verbal reaction totally inexistent?

Has the picture less verisimilitude than the one we first saw?

Note: Ouspensky suggested that points far apart in tridimensional space can touch one another in a further dimension, and that what we know as proximity and separation may appear as affinity and repulsion, sympathy and antipathy.

REALITY AND MANIFESTATION

44 ⸱⁓ *To Be or Not To Be*

ONE: Hello! How are you getting on?

TWO: Pretty rapidly, I think. I have understood a lot recently, and the old ego is getting slimmer every day. One of these fine days I hope to get rid of it altogether.

ONE: You are modest.

TWO: Why?

ONE: You call that getting on rapidly. I call it a miracle.

TWO: How so?

ONE: To reduce, or to get rid of, something that does not exist sounds to me like a chemically-pure miracle.

TWO: It does not exist really, of course; we all know that. The Buddha and his buddhies made that clear. But to us, and as far as we are concerned, it is there all right.

ONE: The Lord Buddha and all his bodhisattvas not only made it clear, they also explained to us how and why it could not exist. How, then, can it be there all right?

TWO: Let us say that it appears to exist. We are thoroughly aware of it.

ONE: We are thoroughly aware of our dream-life when we are dreaming it. Does it exist? We are thoroughly aware of a mirage in the desert. Does that exist? We are thoroughly aware of every mental image we make. Do they exist?

TWO: I see what you mean. It is only an idea.

ONE: Just so, technically referred to—in order to avoid confusion, or perhaps to make it?—as a concept.

TWO: Can you tell me how such a tiresome, foolish, accursed concept ever arose?

ONE: Tiresome and accursed it may be when we are seeking to go beyond it, but foolish it certainly is not.

TWO: How so?

ONE: We may assume it was the first concept we ever had. When first there arose awareness of form, of perceptions, of feelings, impulses, and awareness of awareness itself, known in the East as the skandhas, that awareness became identified with that of which it had become aware. Immediately it assumed attributes and became conditioned. That was the "I-concept." Quite inevitable. Anything but foolish. A necessary element of the life-dream subject to time.

TWO: Necessary to evolution too, I suppose?

ONE: That is an element in the life-dream—perfectly imaginary, like the rest.

TWO: If it was an advance, progress, what is wrong with that?

ONE: Nothing whatsoever. As long as you are content with your dream, it is the very axis of that dream.

TWO: But we are all striving to wake up.

ONE: Those who have that urge *must* strive to wake up.

TWO: Where does the urge come from?

ONE: Reality.

TWO: Their reality?

ONE: There is only reality.

TWO: Why should that concept be particularly false?

ONE: It is not. All concepts are equally false—in the sense

of unreal. But if you succeeded in abandoning all
concepts but that one—you would still not wake up.
That is the concept that keeps you asleep.

TWO: I have been denying its existence as reality, but not as
a reality in my dream. If I can succeed in denying its
existence in any form whatsoever—shall I wake up?

ONE: Even denial implies an assumption, if only an
assumption of something that is unreal.

TWO: So what?

ONE: Of something erroneously conceived nothing whatever that is true can be said.

TWO: So what? So what?

ONE: Stop talking. Act.

TWO: What action can be taken?

ONE: Make the inexistence of an ego a living reality.

TWO: But how?

ONE: How? By non-action, of course. By understanding
that what is not—is not. Only as reality can you act,
and the action of reality is non-action.

45 ⋅- *Kittens in Wool*

It is difficult to doubt that the verbal confusion in which oriental doctrine is delivered to us was intentional. And the
efforts of translators can hardly be said to cut the knots.

Amongst these linguistic muddles perhaps none distresses
us more than the notion of "existence" and "non-existence."
Yet surely it is in itself relatively simple. Regarded from the
point of view of reality—nothing exists. Hui Neng said it—
just like that (the T'ang Masters sometimes spoke simply).
From the point of view of our dream of living, manifestation,
phenomena—everything exists, mirages as well as motor-cars,

saints as they are imagined as well as saints as they lived—for all are mind-products like that which we conceive as "ourselves." Most of these terms have dual meanings, according to the point of view from which they are being used. If we bear that in mind much of the muddle evaporates at once.

Why did the original Sages cultivate linguistic confusion? Why did Jesus say: "I speak in parables so that they may not understand"? When we become sages we shall know.

46 ·— Definitions - II

One has heard it maintained that the current verbal chaos in metaphysical terminology is inevitable, and that we shall never be able to know what anyone means by any technical term until we have become familiar with this manner of thinking. Even if this should be so, one can at least try to put one's own house in order.

The words "I," "we," and the verbs "I am," "we are," *as long as they remain unconditioned* can only refer to reality. Referred to, the clearest term would appear to be "the I-reality."

The word "me," being accusative, can never refer to reality—for that cannot be the object of anything. Therefore "me" must always refer to the concept through which we imagine ourselves to be individuals. Referred to, the clearest term for that illusory entity would seem to be "the I-concept." If one of the numerous terms in current use should be necessary, such as ego, personality, individuality, self, the indefinite article is preferable, since "the" ego implies something that exists, whereas "an" ego does not necessarily imply more than something that might exist, i.e. that, erroneously, is assumed to exist.

The only difficulty would seem to be the necessity for the

inexperienced to distinguish between "I" unconditioned, implying reality, and "I" conditioned as in "I am John Smith," implying the supposed entity so called.

Note: However fully we may realise our inexistence, our unreality as entities, we are still obliged to refer to ourselves as such. The Buddha, it is true, is often recorded as referring to himself as "the Tathagata," and I think the Maharshi may occasionally have spoken of himself as "baghavan," though that may have been playful or as a child may refer to himself as "Tommy," but such a procedure, if it were deliberate, would seem to defeat its own object—for there should be no object. Ramakrishna at one period referred to himself as "this." In our world any such evasion would be merely pretentious. Rather let us freely say "I" (conditioned) and "me," fully savouring the absurdity of such a nonsensical statement, and with a twinkle in our voice only perceptible to, or explicable by, those who can understand.

WORK AND PLAY

47 ~ "L'art Moderne"

People often wonder what "modern" artists mean when they represent human beings in a simplified and apparently distorted manner, as in the case of the famous M. Picasso, and very many others, sincere and insincere. The explanations of the artists themselves are contradictory and often unconvincing to any but their own kind, and indeed it is as unlikely that their rationalised explanation should have any greater value than that of any other category of human beings explaining anything that they do.

One can hardly doubt that what is seeking expression is the reality of a man or a woman conceived as an individual.

Evidently reality has no form, and its expression can only be a symbol, such as plain circle or the Taoist symbol of a circle containing the *Yin* and the *Yang*, but the artist may often be impelled, quite unknown to himself, to seek to express the inherent reality, of which he has an intuition, behind a human being, or, indeed, any animal or object. And that he could not express it in any other manner than by extreme and apparently exaggerated simplification and distortion.

I do not mean to imply that only recently have artists been subjected to this urge or have experienced such an intuition; indeed El Greco very evidently had it, but the artists of classical and Renaissance times were primarily concerned with the soma (physical form) and secondarily with the psyche of their subjects. The deliberate present-day rejection of these factors, or their relegation to a level of subsidiary importance, may have left the way open to a profounder intuition which finds this expression that is so surprising and incomprehensible to the workaday observer.

REALITY AND MANIFESTATION

48 ·– *Between Ourselves*

"One who argues does so because he is confused." (Chuang Tzu)

One who discourses does so because he does not know what to think.

One who knows—only answers questions.

ॐ

When you begin to realise that you are dreaming—what

happens?

You wake up!

❦

A figment of imagination cannot be assumed to have freedom of will.

A figment of imagination cannot be assumed to have a fixed destiny.

A figment of imagination is at the mercy of the imagination that dreams it. But is not all imagination a reaction?

❦

"A man who can forget his own self may be said to have entered the realm of Heaven." (Chuang Tzu)

Questions that Are Not

A good example of a question that is not one is: "Do you believe in such-and-such a thing?" In so far as nothing exists, there is nothing to believe in. In so far as you accept the mind-made universe as relatively real, you cannot disbelieve in anything since everything that mind can imagine can put in an appearance.

WORK AND PLAY

49 ·- Democracy - I

Probably humanity has tried most of the systems of governing itself, but they have nearly all been based on giving power to the qualified, powerful or able. It has been left to present-day humanity to try giving power to the least qualified element within itself, and to erect that attempt into something that resembles a religion.

The sages of all the ages would surely be astonished by the present attempt, if they could know of it, and they would almost certainly point with uniform fingers at the current results which surround us. But such is the power of dogma and propaganda that blindness of faith and blindness of eye combine to impede vision, while the ear listens to the rustling of paper to which has been given a value as fictitious as water in a desert.

Note: Qualification of any kind is usually the prerogative of a minority.

Rule by the unqualified, represented by the ambitious, and by a conflict of greeds, bears no resemblance to the Taoist doctrine of the power of non-action.

Demophily

In contrast to Democracy, Demophily* is the child of good-will and of good sense, and so the grandchild of Love and Wisdom. Realisation of the fundamental maleficence of the former should deepen realisation of the fundamental beneficence of the latter.

---

* *Ed. note:* WWW is here seeking a term to describe the notion of compassionate government based on the concept of the "Sage-ruler" found in the *Tao Te Ching,* as opposed to what he sees as rule by a self-interested, power-backed elite elected via a system offering very limited choice and (perhaps erroneously) termed "democracy."

A genuine demophile (one who profoundly cares for the people) can never be a democrat—for he must desire their total good.

TIME AND SPACE

50 ·~ *Mutt and Jeff*

"Space" only results from seeing things separately and one after the other, a result of our innate inability to have more than one percept at a time. It is a deduction. The notion that there is such a thing, that it exists in itself and of its own right, is absurd!

Space is a concomitant of the process of seeing things independently, indeed of seeing things at all, i.e. of being a spectator, of oneself being separated from oneness. It is therefore dependent on the illusory notion of self.

Space is a supposition for which there is no adequate evidence, of whose existence there is no likelihood, a purely gratuitous complication which obscures a clear vision of reality.

En fin de compte it is just an assumption for which there is no justification whatever. All things considered, it is as big a clown as its compeer—that old lag of the circus of living that we know familiarly as Time.

$$\infty$$

Space is what separates objects. It consists of holes joined together by phenomena. It has no other function than that of keeping things apart. Their apparent apartness depends on this factor, and seems to justify it as an assumption. But if they are seen as one, even for a moment, "space" automatically vanishes, for there is no *place* for it.

❧

TWO: We talk about the phenomenal, and we know what it
means, but what does it really amount to in practice?
What are its limits, its real significance?

ONE: Press a button—and there's nothing to be seen
anywhere.

WORK AND PLAY

51 · "Progress"

One of the most widespread illusions of mankind is the
assumption that whatever novelty he introduces is necessarily an "improvement." In the present age mankind is suffering
from a fever of change: nearly nothing can be left as it was,
nearly everything must be altered, and ever more rapidly—
and the alteration is nearly always assumed to be an
"improvement."

At the same time one observes that the contrary is generally the opinion of the cultured minority, the new way is
found to be longer, further, more wearisome, the new thing is
seen as clumsy, ugly, ill-made, the new schedule almost
invariably more inconvenient. In seeking to extract more
money from some people others are displeased and
incommoded, colossal injustices are inflicted on some in the
supposed interests of others. Meanwhile nature is ever more
disfigured by man who fancies that whatever he does is
"better."

Inevitably both points of view are equally insensate, for
both are illusory evaluations. The "old" was once "new,"
change from what was before, and the "new" will shortly be

"old" and subject to further change, whereas the ideas of convenience and beauty are resultants of habit.

The most that one can say is that nothing man has ever done, is doing, or ever will do can be other than a disfigurement of nature, of that nature of which he himself is an integral part.

REALITY AND MANIFESTATION
52 ·~ Impasse

As long as we continue speaking of "the" ego, time and space, thereby making mental images of them, each one a concept, as though such things existed, and despite intellectual conviction regarding their unreality—we are never likely to leap over the then almost insuperable barrier that lies across our path.

How to realise the veritable inexistence of these notions, that they are not phenomenal (relative) reality at all? That is not easy and is vigorously resisted by the self-identified aspect of mind. Rare are those who will face it: usually people will not even listen, or their attention is only a polite pretence. But in these observations I have tried numerous lines of approach—for this requires intuition rather than reasoning for its apprehension.

Perhaps it is necessary to *ask*, perhaps it is necessary that the vital information shall be in reply to a question, to an urge, in order that the intuition may successfully be communicated?

Let us remember: "the" ego, time and space are really symbols—like algebra, technical apparatus of the intellect devised in order *provisionally* to explain an anomaly. They are convenient hypotheses—like the "aether."

❦

This understanding has never been easy in any civilisation; probably in no other has it been so difficult or rare, surrounded as we are from birth by people so firmly convinced of the reality of their individual entity. Every element of our civilisation is based on this supposition, every aspect of our lives is permeated by it. Personality is a cult, and the evils that surround us are the direct result of the development of this assumption.

Even an intellectual understanding of the inexistence of our "selves" is a rare and bitter attainment which few even attempt. And that is only the elimination round which qualifies us for access to Reality.

Note: Intellectual understanding should not be indispensable to a simple "mind," but, with our conditioning, it would seem to be an almost inevitable preliminary.

Need we wonder. . . .

53 ✦ *The Mind Is a Moon*

The "mind" is a moon: it has no light of its own: it is lit by the sun.

Everything you behold by "moonlight" is lit by the sun. Everything you behold by "mindlight" is lit by the Ultimate Subject—that is the whole world of appearance, all manifestation.

The "mind" is a reflected force-field and its force is the Subject. An eye cannot see itself, nor can the mind conceive the force by which it conceives. When that force is directly experienced the mindlight is obscured as is the moonlight when the sun shines directly. When the sun shines the moon-mind loses all its importance and its activities become inconspicuous and innocuous. The reflected force-field fades in the light of the real.

The Day of Pseudo-Glory

In a pre-Columbian religion it is recorded that a young man chosen for sacrifice was accorded one day during which he was treated like a prince. He was dressed in gorgeous robes, given everything generally considered desirable, and was the object of universal acclamation. He enjoyed every prerogative of a prince except the power to do anything whatsoever.

Was this not a symbol of man set up as an individual, a separate self, an ego, an independent personality? For his day of life as such he imagines himself an independent being, possessing free-will and all sorts of "rights" and dignities ("la dignité humaine," "la personne humaine," "the rights of man," "liberty," "justice," and all that clap-trap), and he never notices that, as an individual—he has exactly no power whatever to do anything whatsoever except glory in his illusory situation. Both are puppets, for neither has any existence at all as what he imagines that he is.

Hard words?

54 · Karma: A Suggestion

One wonders whether "bad *karma*" may not be the result of seeking to run off the tracks of one's destiny (one's destiny being the force of circumstances which motivates each psycho-somatic apparatus), and "good karma" the result of adhering stolidly to those tracks, rather than the performance of actions that are assumed to be "good" or "bad" in themselves?

The latter notion is primary and *simpliste*, let us say naïve, and it might in fact be possible apparently to do, or to do on a parallel plane, an action other than that which we have to do since it already exists. Such a deviation, even if only apparent or on a parallel plane, should merit punishment, if there be such a thing, whereas living strictly in accordance with reality should bring its own reward.

To do what one has to do with eyes wide open and without hesitation—that surely is right action. To attempt to do, and apparently to do, what one has not to do, is surely wrong action. Is that not the only morality that is real?

⁂

Is suffering anything but seeking or desiring to do otherwise than one must? Is the avoidance of suffering anything but sensing what one must do—and just doing it? Is suffering anything but trying to live on a plane other than that on which our destiny *immanquablement* lies?

If we deliberately attempt to live on a plane other than that on which our destiny lies—it is reasonable that we should suffer for it until, inevitably, we return to our own and live in accordance with the "nature of things," i.e. our own nature.

Free-will - V

An action is extended in Space and Time. Since both are merely symbols, like algebra, an action may be said to *exist* but not to be *performed*. Therefore it could not be possible voluntarily to perform, or avoid performing, any action, since it already exists, or does not exist, in reality.

TIME AND SPACE

55 ·~ *Dualism Is Duodimensional*

The run-way lights are seen one after the other before an aeroplane leaves the ground, i.e. while it is on a plane-surface of two dimensions. When it leaves the ground and circles the aerodrome in a third dimension (height) the run-way lights are all seen apparently at once.

Probably all dualisms can be conceived as duodimensional, i.e. as on a plane-surface, more usefully than just as "opposites" or "complementaries," their reality being that which they are seen to be from a third right-angle of measurement. Thus Past and Future can be conceived as on a plane-surface, like the lights the aeroplane passes by on the run-way, whereas the Present is that totality wherein Past and Future are seen at once from "above" or the dimension at right-angles.

The Present is in another direction of measurement from those in which lie the Past and the Future.

☙

Could it be that a function of our psyche has remained confined to two dimensions, and that our conceptual faculty has not yet invaded that domain and brought to it tridimensional vision?

At any rate the application of a further right-angled direction of measurement to Past and Future, or to any other pair of opposite-complementaries, such as Life-Death,

Good-Evil, Reality-Phenomena, should result in unicity of vision—*which is perhaps all that we need*—if we could see how that is to be done.

ॐ

By diverse lines of thought one finds oneself again and again facing the conclusion that full enlightenment, awakening, is in this context simply access to the use of a further direction of measurement of vision.

Note: It has been observed previously, perhaps more than once, that there is no such thing as the "present." The phrase "Past, Present and Future" is a figure of speech. Phenomenally we only know Past and Future—and Future only when it is already Past, the so-called Present being an entirely imaginary line of demarcation no more trace of which exists than there does a line of longitude, latitude or the equator.

The "Present" is a concept applicable only to the timeless state of the Awakened.

Time

The Past is a memory, i.e. an idea, an object of consciousness. The Future is an image, another idea, another object of consciousness. The Present, which we never know until it is Past, is therefore also an idea, a notion, an object of consciousness. None of them is real, each is imaginary. Time does not exist.

The eternal present, the now-moment, the interval between thoughts, which we normally never perceive, alone is real.

56 ·- *Débris - III*

I am—all the time. I am not this and that: this and that are never I.

❧

Nothing is mine (possessed by me): I am everything.

❧

The individual is apparent but inexistent—like the reflection of the moon in puddle.

❧

Buddhism is a way of life? Is it not also a way out of life?

❧

Surely the simple fact of consciousness is Consciousness Itself and Reality?

The fact of being conscious is being, is real, is the only self there is.

❧

The only you is what you do.

There is no doer: only an action.

How could there be an actor and action? Action involves time, and there is no one to act.

Therefore action itself is actor.

Definitions - III

Past and Future are a duality of which Present is the reality. The now-moment alone is eternal and real.

༄

Satori is a concept: how could it exist?

REALITY AND MANIFESTATION

57 ·- Us

TWO: Will you answer a straight question in a straight manner?

ONE: Only if it *is* a question. I warn you—they are rare.

TWO: What do you mean by that?

ONE: Most so-called questions carry their own answers in their pockets. Of the rest the majority are like the one suggested by Hubert Benoit: "Why does the Eiffel Tower go for a walk in the skies of Paris every morning at 8 o'clock?"

TWO: Mine is neither. It is simply: if there is any known method of transcending the ego, which, in your opinion, is the best?

ONE: *The ego?* Whatever do you mean? There is no such thing. Your question is an Eiffel Tower walking in the sky.

TWO: I mean, of course, "what we conceive as an ego."

ONE: That is exactly like what you conceive as the Man in the Moon. But there isn't one.

TWO: Then why do we think we know it so well?

ONE: We don't know it, well or badly: we just imagine it.

TWO: And yet it is the supreme barrier between us and reality?

ONE: Not the supreme: the one and only.

TWO: How incredibly difficult it all is!

ONE: Difficult? It is all as simple and obvious and evident as somebody's nose.

TWO: Could you be persuaded to justify that?

ONE: By all means. We are brought up—by parents, schoolmasters, even university professors (who might know better)—to believe that the world around us, all that is perceived by our six—I said six—senses, is real, and that what is not so perceived is unreal. But from the earliest recorded times wise men, men who deeply considered such matters, have realised that the opposite is the truth. That which is sensorially perceived is phenomenal; whereas reality is sensorially imperceptible.

TWO: Nowadays we all know that. Even some men of science, the top ones of course.

ONE: The "we" you refer to have always known that.

TWO: Noumenon and phenomena—the basic dualism. Is that what you mean? Or Subject and object, Cause and effect?

ONE: Words only mean what you wish them to mean. Ultimate Subject and objects, Initial Cause and effects, may serve in suitable contexts, but more particularly Pure Consciousness and objects of consciousness, all dualistic. Have I justified my statement that it is all as simple and obvious and evident as a nose?

TWO: No, you have not. What has that platitude—for I think I may call it that?—got to do with the so-called "ego"?

ONE: I am glad you see it as a platitude, for a platitude is something you no longer doubt, and the rest is all contained therein—in the waistcoat pocket of that platitude.

TWO: Then please turn out the pocket.

ONE: Reality and phenomena, Subject and objects, Cause and effects, are dualistic complementaries, neither can exist except by reference to the other, or, if you prefer, relatively. That of which they are the dual aspect we cannot know, or conceive as we say, for that alone IS, and that alone we ARE—and an eye cannot see itself; but we can consign a word to it, such as Non-Being, the Principle of Consciousness, or just Tao—though all words are ultimately dualistic.

TWO: That seems sound doctrine, and so? . . .

ONE: When we say "We are" the only adjective we can use is one such as those just suggested—Reality, Subject or Cause, and, of course, its complementary.

TWO: We are Reality and phenomena, Subject and objects, Cause and effects?

ONE: Yes—and *phenomena are merely derivative.*

TWO: So I-as-phenomenon am merely derivative?

ONE: Of course, but even so not just one phenomenon, object, or effect, but all phenomena, objects, effects.

TWO: I see. Well?

ONE: Well what?

TWO: How does that affect *me?*

ONE: You are Subject-"I" and all objects, not just the body and mind, the psycho-somatic apparatus you were brought up to believe that you were.

TWO: So that as a psycho-somatic apparatus I only exist as a phenomenon, an object, an effect?

ONE: Just so—as an object of consciousness and *not* as a

conscious object.

TWO: Please go on.

ONE: Why, no phenomenon, effect, or object of consciousness could possibly itself have consciousness! A shadow cannot have substance: it is only a projection. It is a derivation; of itself it is nothing, has nothing, can do nothing whatever.

TWO: So I cannot even think?

ONE: As an object of consciousness of course you cannot! The moon cannot give light of itself. There is only one sun in the solar-system.

TWO: And that sun is the Principle of Consciousness, or Tao?

ONE: Exactly, call it what you will—for, being IT and nothing else, we cannot conceive IT.

TWO: Then It perceives and conceives dualistically as us? Subject-us, of course.

ONE: I know of no other valid interpretation of being.

TWO: And what we perceive and conceive to be a psychosomatic apparatus is just an apparatus activated by Subject-us, seeming to be conscious by our consciousness, seeming to live by our life, kept alight and in motion by our current?

ONE: Just so.

TWO: "We" can do nothing, think nothing, know nothing, by or of ourselves as psycho-somatic apparatus, because we don't exist as such, in our own right, at all, but only as a reflection of the One light which alone we ARE?

ONE: Yes, but remember, one reflection is no more or less US than any other—all reflections are equally and together reflections of US.

TWO: So that there is nothing that could be an "I" (or an

"ego") except I-Principle-of-Consciousness?

ONE: That is so, though, dualistically conceived, we can know ourselves as Subject and objects, Observer and all that is observed, which is the only identification that is both real and dualistically conceivable. *That* identification dissolves the so-called "ego" once and for all.

TWO: Perhaps, after all, it is less complicated than I had thought.

ONE: Less? Where is there any complication? How could it possibly be otherwise? Nothing else could make sense. Therefore it is simple—as I told you. Did not the Maharshi tell you?

TWO: Now that I come to think of it I believe he did, but I didn't hoist it in. I feel I must take it for a walk. Good night. The moon is full and one can see miles by moonlight.

ONE: Good night. But when you look at the moon don't forget where the light comes from—that you too are a moon! Moons, all moons. . . .

WORK AND PLAY

58 ·- Let It Grow

All complementaries are interdependent, and so fundamentally in harmony. It is we who render them conflicting. The element of struggle, the notion of overcoming opposition, of conquest, is illusory. There is nothing to conquer, and therefore nothing to fight.

Government, or anything else, by conflict, instead of by co-operation, by discord instead of by harmony, is fundamentally absurd. If men who understood that exercised power, a major cause of human misery would no longer operate.

It follows that purpose has no place in a relative world, since there is nothing to be overcome. Nothing has an "aim," nothing is achieving anything in reality, *in fact nothing is moving.* That is just illusion which proceeds from the dualistic outlook that creates the notion of Time.

The *Baghavad Gita* insists that work must be performed for its own sake and not for its result. The *Tao Te Ching* and Zen say the same thing. Taoism, Advaita, Mahayana—all know it, all say that in their own way.

"Let it grow," leave things alone, no achievement or victory could be real that is a victory or an achievement rather than an inevitable result, something that naturally occurs. Forcing is just fighting the waves with a sword, empty gesture, fatuous and futile.

REALITY AND MANIFESTATION

59 ·~ *The Second Barrier*

We have said that the words of the Masters are to be taken literally, and that our basic error is to continue to regard the concept of an "ego" as something that nevertheless exists— "for us," or however we choose to try to justify our retention of the notion.

Another, and vital, error of the same kind is to ignore, as we nearly all seem to do, the insistence of the Masters, in Zen and in Advaita, that there is nothing to "realise" and no one to "realise" anything, that there is nothing to strive after or grasp, and no one to do either—and for obvious enough reasons. The Buddha himself stated categorically in the Diamond Sutra that he had acquired nothing by complete and perfect enlightenment. Glance around us—who is paying attention to that? Individuals and schools—almost exclusively engaged in doing exactly the opposite by every means that they can hear of or devise!

The Maharshi suggested that the trouble may arise through the word "realise"; it is a verb, and the last syllable implies action of some kind. But no action is possible, and to try to take any defeats its own object. It means "to make or render or become real," but that which is real in us is so already, always was and always will be. We can no more "become" real than we can become ourselves. What, may one ask, could "we," objects of consciousness (*not* conscious objects), electronic machines, force-fields in perpetual flux, psycho-somatic apparatuses—whatever image we may choose—"do" in such a matter? What a nonsensical notion! We who are already real, and only real, have no action to take in order to be what we are! No action is possible in reality; it is permanent and already real*ised*. Do we have to realise that we have a nose? True, we aren't bothered, in the latter case, with the notion that we haven't one, as we are, in the former case, with the notion that we aren't real—or real*ised*, as we say it. But the latter notion is even more absurd than the former would be—for our noses, obvious as they are, are still less obvious than our reality—which underlies every thought or action that we attribute to ourselves.

True, also, our noses may be objects of consciousness, whereas our reality could never be—I have explained that several times—and so we cannot know our reality objectively, as we can know objectively our noses, but our reality is nevertheless a certainty. It is the ultimate certainty, of which nobody who uses the first person singular or plural can possibly doubt without thereby flatly contradicting himself, a certainty ever present that can never be objectivised in any circumstances but of which nevertheless we can be conscious at any and every moment.

60 ·– Spontaneity – I

Spontaneity by-passes the processes of the conceptual (aspect of) mind.

Our ubiquitous error lies in mistaking concepts for reality, for instance our idea of a body—which is only an idea—for an actual body. There is absolutely no reason to suppose that the reality it may have bears any resemblance to our concept.

That which we perceive is a projection and not a thing-in-itself. That, surely, is what the Buddha meant when he told us, in the Diamond Sutra, that we should not cherish the notion of things having intrinsic qualities or not having intrinsic qualities—for "qualities," or their absence, are notions, concepts, projected on to "things."

Spontaneity is no more under "our" control than is our blood-pressure, but by understanding the unreality of concepts in general and of the body-concept in particular the way for spontaneity should be laid open.

But spontaneity is clearly the aim of the Zen Masters and is the explanation of almost everything recorded of them in word or in act.

❧

Reintegration with Nature, which we are, is the recovery of spontaneity.

61 ·– Will – I

Will is an imaginary function of an imaginary entity.

Will – II

As ultimate Reality we can have no will, for Non-Being is devoid of attributes.

As relative Reality, in the dualist aspect of Consciousness and objects of Consciousness, Observer and all that is observed, we are integrated in the Cosmos and act accordingly.

As individuals we are merely figments and cannot have will other than as desire and its opposite.

Will, therefore, is just a figure of speech.

Will – III

We are like passengers in a railway-train who think that we can change our mind and make the train go anywhere we wish.

62 ·– Seeking for Satori

Every time you seek Enlightenment you lose it.

You had it, though you were not aware of it, but when you sought it you inevitably turned away from it.

Whenever we start to search for something we have not lost we always necessarily separate ourselves from it.

Spiritual Experience

When I hear people speaking of experiences ("spiritual" understood) that they have had, or that some other, envied, person has had, and which appear to imply some kind of preliminary or try-out of Satori, I invariably wonder what on earth they are talking about; and with such earnestness—for slightly hushed voices are often invoked. Such experiences, since they are recognised as such, are evidently experiences in time and are therefore inapplicable to a context which implies reality. Neither Satori nor any other spiritual state could be in Time, nor, not being in Time, could be an experience.

Suchness

The Void (sunyata) is called emptiness because it cannot be an object of knowledge (or consciousness). That is, it is only empty to us as subject for whom every percept is object. This rendering as "emptiness" has caused endless confusion—for "Void" is not that at all, but, on the contrary, Reality Itself.

It is the hypostasis of the opposites, the dimensional extension of linear contradictions, or their "inner" identity, i.e. the identity which becomes apparent when their extension in a further dimension is perceived.

63 ⋅~ There Is No "I" but I—A Causerie

I

All we can know about Reality is that it must be eternal, informal and non-dual. Since our intellectual apparatus is subject to the concepts of time, space and duality it is thereby incapable of knowing that to which those concepts are inapplicable. Therefore it is only by by-passing the intellectual apparatus that we can have any cognisance of Reality, and such cognisance cannot be expressed in language, because that is a purely intellectual medium.

For instance we can know that we are Reality; in a sense we cannot not know it; but it is not demonstrable.

We can understand that everything must be real, but that, at the same time, nothing we can perceive sensorially can possibly be an accurate representation of what it is in reality, for everything we can perceive is in a time, space and dualistic context, that is to say: it is subject to duration, has form in space, and is one part of a dualistic concept—itself and not-itself—whereas its reality, the thing-in-itself, its suchness, must be eternal (without time), formless (without space) and unitary (without duality), and as such we are unable to know it. Moreover we are only able to perceive it at all by clothing it in qualities—such as size, weight, colour, shape, each of which is a function of its own opposite, and an arbitrary point on a scale limited by the restricted range of our senses, and which therefore has no intrinsic reality but is merely a sensorial estimation.

Thus everything we perceive is only an interpretation in a dualistic, temporal and formal framework, of a suchness, a reality which we are unable to know. Were we able to know the reality of anything at all, we may surmise that it could only appear to us as something such as a mathematical or algebraical symbol.

Many of us realise this well enough, but fewer have understood that what we regard as ourselves are also objects that we perceive, subject to the same conditions of perception as everything else. If we strip ourselves, our friends and our dogs, of the names, functions and qualities we clothe them with, nothing remains but our suchness—which cannot be represented otherwise than, just possibly, by a mathematical symbol. Let us not forget that the image which "strikes" a retina only produces chemical changes therein, and that these changes, transmitted by nerve-impulses, only effect corresponding chemical changes in cerebral matter, the resulting image being merely an *interpretation* in consciousness of chemical changes in that cerebral matter. To suppose that anything really *is* (is in timeless, formless Reality) that which it *appears* (as an interpretation, in a space-time context, of chemical changes in matter)—is surely the limit of absurdity! At the same time the image that "strikes" a retina is itself the projection of that image in consciousness, as is any such image when we dream it, and is not anything external—for nothing can be external to consciousness.

So much for what we *aren't!* But what *are* we? Strange as it may seem to us—who have been thinking that we are what we think we see in a looking-glass—we are reality. Just that, and nothing else whatever. If we could get that into our heads our troubles surely would be over.

II

Is it not enough? It is. It should be. But we may like to try to understand how it comes about and how it works.

Everything sensorially perceived, by our senses or by mechanical extensions thereof, the entire perceptible universe, *including what we are used to regarding as ourselves,* is an interpretation of reality in consciousness. Psychologically the perceptible universe may be regarded as a projection, apparently exterior to consciousness, of images from within consciousness, but we know that there can be nothing exterior to consciousness, so that the formula of psychology may be regarded as technical jargon based on the misunderstanding that we are separate from the universe we appear to perceive. This is, of course, the basic illusion, which bars the way to enlightenment.

Is that still not enough? It is. It should be. Why does it not seem to be enough? Something is missing? What can it be? Ourselves? Why, of course. But we don't exist as separate entities. The Buddha told us so dozens of times, the T'ang Masters told us so, the Upanishads told us so, down to and including our contemporary, who lived in the awakened state for fifty years, Ramana Maharshi. We weren't able to believe them. Or perhaps we thought we believed them, but secretly did not, because we were not able to see how it could be so, how we could not be what it seemed to us so obvious that we were. And, indeed, to believe is *not* enough. We must *know* it to be so. And then all that remains is to *experience* that it is so.

But now we have seen, and how simply, that it not only can be so, but must be so, and in fact *is* so!

We have realised that we are reality, and nothing else whatever, and that all that we perceive, including that which we imagined was ourselves, are just objects in consciousness, interpretations of reality in a dualistic medium, all of them ultimately ourselves of course, a waking dream in no essential dissimilar from the dreams of our sleep.

What a relief it is to know that there is no "I" but I! Is it not the greatest discovery possible to man? Is any comparable thrill imaginable? To believe it is a little; to know it is much; but until it is experienced the illusion holds full sway. Then even gravity is no more!

❧

Is somebody still asking who it is who is looking at his

reflection in the looking-glass, who is talking, who is listening? As the Maharshi might have said—how many "who's" have you? It is you of course, or me, and there is only one of us, and that is a real one. We are all in it, all nature and everything that is. That is the overwhelming, ubiquitous reality that we are. It is we who are looking and talking and listening, but what we see and hear are objects in consciousness—in looking-glasses also—just dream-figments, what we now see as electronic force-fields in flux imagined as individuals and serving as media for the dualistic objectivisation of reality as consciousness and the objects thereof.

PHYSICS AND METAPHYSICS

64 ·~ Life: A Definition

What we know as a "life"
is the analytical realisation
in the seriality of time
of our eternal reality.

65 ·~ The Opposites and Complementaries

No doubt the characteristics of the famous pairs of opposites have been studied by someone fully qualified, but, judging by the vagueness and confusion with which they are treated in nearly all contemporary literature, few people have troubled to do it or have been able to find the work of the qualified, if it exists.

Herewith is an attempted analysis, the results of which are surely suggestive and would upset a number of apple-carts if applied.

A. Complementaries co-exist: both must be present at one time and place. They are absolute in the sense of not being relative points on a scale. For instance:

Obverse and reverse
Positive and negative
Right and left
Subject and object

B. Opposites are mutually exclusive and cannot co-exist (at one time and place); i.e. when one appears its opposite disappears. These are relative in the sense of being points on a scale. For instance:

Light and dark
Hot and cold
Heavy and light
Good and evil
Love and hate
Joy and sorrow
Pleasure and pain

C. Only "things" and their contraries are pure pairs of opposites. For instance:

Being and non-being
Self and not-self

All categories are mutually dependent, are a function each of the other.

Note: It is an error to regard one element of "B" as Positive and the other as Negative: that they can never be. The two categories "A" and "B" are incompatible, at right-angles, i.e. of a different direction of measurement. "A" alone has polarity.

66 ·- *Subject and Object*

Therefore:

Subject must always have object—perceived as objects.

There are no objects anywhere at any moment that are not integral in their subject.

All objects have only one subject.

Subject and consciousness are one.

Objects are the consciousness of their subject.

Objects have no consciousness other than the consciousness which is their subject, and of which they are.

An object only exists figuratively, a single object is an aspect of objects, its apparent separation being a limitation of perception.

All objects are one, and they are subject.

Such is the dualistic aspect of Reality.

REALITY AND MANIFESTATION

67 ·- *Free-will - VI*

Objects can have no "free-will": they can have no "will" of any kind, for they are only an aspect of subject, but the energy which constitutes their appearance may be misapplied and be expended ineffectually and in opposition to the inevitable sequence of events in time and space. This inconsequent struggling may be misconstrued as "will."

Subject, as pure reality, is free from constraint, but as one element of a dualism it is conditioned by the other element thereof, which is its object. Dualistically, therefore, it is not "free."

There is no "free-will" in duality.

There is no "predestination" in reality.

❧

When you manifest what is known as a "will" you are thereby identified with your object.

Can any distinction be made between the figment that is called a "will" and the figment that is called an "ego"?

68 ·~ What Am I?

TWO: Great news, old chap, the greatest ever.

ONE: Excellent. That is to say?

TWO: I am reality!

ONE: As obvious as your nose, but congratulations on noticing it.

TWO: But it is terrific! I had no idea life held such a thrill! I want to dance, or jump over the moon. I feel as if a fog had lifted, as though an insupportable burden had been lifted from my shoulders.

ONE: The I-concept is like being gagged, and bound with chains, is it not?

TWO: Yes, indeed. I had long believed the thing did not exist, but now I have come to know it. What a difference!

ONE: "Believing" it was only the usual pretence; *knowing* it is still intellectual; when you *experience* it even gravity will no longer exist.

TWO: When I look, when I speak, when I listen, it is reality that looks and speaks and listens!

ONE: Who else could there be to look and speak and listen?

TWO: No one, but I didn't realise it. And what I see, what

I say, what I hear—is reality!

ONE: Nonsense; it is nothing of the kind!

TWO: What do you mean? What is it then?

ONE: What you see, say or hear is only an interpretation of reality in a dualistic medium, and bears no recognisable resemblance to reality except in its suchness which can neither be seen, said nor heard.

TWO: And yet the "I" that sees, speaks, listens, is reality? It seems illogical.

ONE: Reality knows nothing of logic; it has never been to school.

TWO: Even so . . . But of course you must be right; come to think of it, what I see, say and hear could not be really real, could it?

ONE: It could not. What you see, say and hear consists of objects in consciousness, interpretations of reality in a context of time, space and duality.

TWO: Yes, yes, but why?

ONE: Because, of course, reality being outside time, without space, and non-dual—all of which are concepts only—cannot be perceived as it is via those limitations.

TWO: Then how can I really perceive?

ONE: You cannot—unless as an algebraic symbol, or, perhaps, as relation, as harmony for instance; you are normally seen as an object in consciousness, dualistically in time, and spatially as form.

TWO: My reality, my suchness, can only be inferred?

ONE: The inference is inescapable, but your suchness is imperceptible.

TWO: How, then, do I become perceptible?

ONE: By being clothed; you yourself are invisible, only your clothes are seen.

TWO: My clothes? What clothes, and where do they come from?

ONE: Your clothes are qualities, projected on to you by dualistic thinking.

TWO: What kind of qualities?

ONE: All kinds—size, weight, shape, colour, character. . . .

TWO: But those are all estimations, functions of their opposites, points on a scale of imaginary values, limited by the range of our sense, devoid of intrinsic reality!

ONE: You see that clearly; you have been reading the Diamond Sutra—"Thus have I heard. . . ."

TWO: And stripped of these arbitrary and unreal dualistic estimations, what am I?

ONE: A hole in space.

TWO: Like everything else?

ONE: Like everything else sensorially perceptible. Like the whole universe as perceived by our senses and their mechanical extensions.

TWO: The suchness of no object can ever be perceived?

ONE: Obviously not.

TWO: But what are objects, when all is said and done?

ONE: Objectivisations of reality in the only way reality can be objectivised, that is, by the dualistic approach, comprising consciousness and objects thereof—all of which we are.

TWO: And consciousness includes all objects?

ONE: Everything that is cognisable. Nothing is outside consciousness, for there is no outside of that.

TWO: As subject, I am always real; as object, I am always relative?

ONE: Relativity meaning reality envisaged dualistically as Observer and observed.

TWO: Suddenly it seems simple!

ONE: Complications only arise in false problems.

TWO: How is it possible to identify oneself with an object, when one knows oneself as the subject?

ONE: It is not possible! You have been identifying yourself with an object instead of recognising yourself as being *also* the subject, that is all.

TWO: And yet I was eternally saying "I," like everybody else!

ONE: That "I" was an object, never the real subject when you used it conditionally, that is the reason.

TWO: So that is it; when one understands, realises, knows that one is I-reality . . . it becomes obvious!

ONE: As obvious as a nose!

69 ~ The Fact of the Matter

Is not the essential problem contained in this proposition: whereas, as reality, we are necessarily the duality of subject and all its objects in consciousness, we have become identified with an object only? As a result each *object* has the illusion that it is a *subject*—which it can never be. This error is the so-called "ego."

It should only be necessary to rectify this false perspective by recognising ourselves as subject and all its objects, which is our reality.

Only? Impossible as long as we regard the world via that identification and speak as from objects as though they were subjects; quite possible if we reject the identification and look and speak as the unconditioned "I," which is the reality that we necessarily are.

Note: "We" is always reality speaking, but as soon as it is conditioned it speaks subject to time, space and duality.

70 ·- *Definition of Spontaneity*

Spontaneity is just acting directly—direct action on the part of the reality that we are, instead of indirect action that is action attributed to the instrument that transmits it.

The instrument, the psycho-somatic apparatus, carries out the action subject to the concepts of time, space and duality, which are its limitations, but the action alone exists, there is no actor (as has so often been pointed out), and the "onlie begetter" of the action is our reality.

Such indirect action, normal action, is necessarily cumbersome, and frequently ineffectual, thoughts so transmitted in words are tortuous and ultimately untrue, but the act of the action and the meaning behind the words are real and ours—for the instrument is only an intermediary.

When we, as subject, speak or act directly, still via an instrument but not attributing to that instrument the authorship of the action or of the idea, which can only be ours—that is what we know as spontaneity.

Note: It is understood that the apparatus-object is an element of the full duality of subject-objects in consciousness, which we are in the dualistic aspect of Reality. But the subject, not the object, initiates action.

71 ⸱⁓ *The Last Lap*

ONE: Hello! How are you?

TWO: In the dumps.

ONE: Re-identified?

TWO: I often forget my reality.

ONE: There is an Italian proverb which can be helpful to the absent-minded. It says, "If someone tells you that your nose is gone, put up your hand to see." Try it.

TWO: It is there.

ONE: Where else could it be?

TWO: Discouraging, all the same.

ONE: Not at all. Knowing is just getting a grip on something, not final installation therein. We must be penetrated by understanding right down to the rock-bottom of ourselves, for knowing drives the false identification before it until finally it drives it out. It is like the fox and its fleas.

TWO: How so?

ONE: The fox is said to back slowly upstream into a river while his fleas crowd forward trying to keep dry. When they are all collected on his nose, he dips it— and they all float off down to the sea!

TWO: Yet I have understood, for when I hear or read of somebody thinking as from an object I immediately perceive his error.

ONE: Each such perception is a nail in the coffin of your own habit of identification.

TWO: When the habit is overcome, is abandoned, I shall remain in the bliss of my first realisation of the real nature of the so-called "ego," that it is only the absurd attribution of subjectivity to one object?

ONE: No, that was excitement, not bliss!

TWO: Then what? . . .

ONE: You have only half understood. Ceasing to mistake an object for subject, no longer attributing subjectivity to an object, does not take you out of dualism.

TWO: But in so doing I know myself as subject and all objects.

ONE: Quite so: that is the dualistic aspect of reality, that which we really are in the relative reality of daily life. That too must be transcended if we would know our real nature which you describe, decently enough, as bliss.

TWO: In order to transcend dualism we must transcend the dualistic aspect of reality?

ONE: Evidently. It is as subject-creating objects, that is, creating the apparent universe, that we exist dualistically or relatively.

TWO: So that getting rid of the false I-concept is just clearing the path?

ONE: That constitutes an insuperable barrier while it subsists. Do not minimise the importance of its dissolution.

TWO: And how does one set about the final transcendence?

ONE: I can only give you my own suppositions, the advice of a fellow pilgrim. I think the Masters both knew and told us. Have a look and see what they said.

TWO: The Buddha, Huang Po, Hui Neng, the *Upanishads,* the *Gita,* Shankara, Padma Sambhava, Maharshi?

ONE: Any one should suffice, but different forms of words and metaphors stimulate the *buddhi* in different people according to their background and wealth of ignorance. Sometimes even a feebly pointing finger may happen to indicate the moon.

TWO: In your view what did they suggest?

ONE: They all suggested the abandonment of intellection or mentation—thinking, image-making, conceptualism.

TWO: How can we in daily life?

ONE: In the external aspect of daily life perhaps we cannot—altogether. Perhaps even the Maharshi couldn't. But in our inner life—why not?

TWO: What takes the place of that?

ONE: Could it be spontaneity?

TWO: Is that not just constant recollection of our reality?

ONE: Your intuition sounds to me like genuine *buddhi*. Shall we try it?

TWO: And that is the last lap?

ONE: There are no laps. There are just paths to the precipice. Then comes the jump.

DÉBRIS

72 ˑ Enlightenment

Every phenomenon that exists is a creation of thought.
                    HUANG PO, *Wan Ling Record,* 6*

Since Reality alone exists immutable, and objects do not—who is there to experience enlightenment? It cannot exist either.

Enlightenment is neither more, nor is it less, than our reality itself.

---

* *Ed. note:* from "The Zen Teaching of Huang Po" by John Blofeld—p. 72

Spontaneity – II

Spontaneity is being present in the present.

Presence in the present, seizing the present, if only for an instant, is spontaneity.

Personalised Deity

To anyone firmly identified with a supposed "ego"—God is necessarily his supreme enemy, and the embodiment of injustice.

But blaming God is like blaming the sun for not shining.

Transcending Dualism

It is as subject-creating objects that we exist dualistically. In order to transcend dualism we must transcend the dualistic aspect of our reality.

Ceasing to mistake the object for subject only destroys the false identification which is the notion that the object itself is "I"—it does carry one out of duality.

Show a Leg!

When a friend or a child has a nightmare one tries to awaken him; often one has to shake him or thump him in order to bring this about.

And yet we wonder and are shocked when we read that the Zen Masters treated their pupils so roughly, using these same methods to the same end!

73 ·~ *Who Are We?—A Causerie*

Huang Po makes an unusually categorical statement according to the *Wan Ling Record*. He says textually: "A perception, sudden as blinking, that subject and object are one, will lead to a deeply mysterious wordless understanding; and by this understanding will you awake to the truth of Zen."

Evidently in our consciousness, dualistically divided, we know ourselves as subject and object, as positive and negative, as *yang* and *yin* (as the Chinese put it), and since we are unable to be conscious of more than one thought at a time we have to recognise these dual aspects of ourselves *consecutively*, and can never recognise them together, which indeed is the mechanism of duality. Yet Huang Po tells us, I think we may say reminds us, that they are not divided in reality, that they are one, and that to realise that unity in an intuition—since we are unable to realise it as a concept—is to realise our reality.

How simple it appears!

Perhaps it is? What, in fact, is hindering us from experiencing this essential intuition? Surely just the concept whereby we think of our objective aspect as subject? That is an erroneous identification, for subject and object are one but object is not subject when experienced dualistically, and that error is responsible for the notion of an "ego" which all the Masters told us does not exist.

Suppose we reverse the identification and think of our subjective aspect as object? We just cannot! For an eye cannot see itself, nor can an "I": subject cannot see itself as object—for ultimately subject is pure consciousness, absolute and unique. Reversing an erroneous identification could only replace one error by another. That is why all that is required is the abolition of the identification.

In order to abolish an identification it should suffice to realise that it is erroneous. If we see and know that the object cannot ever at any moment be its subject in duality, we can no longer admit that it is so, or that such a thing as an "ego" can exist.

The misplaced identification abolished, who are we?

Who can we be but the ultimate subject, non-dual consciousness in which the duality of subject and objects becomes manifest dualistically?

Do not let us be hypnotised by the word "subject," etymologically absurd, to which an arbitrary and contradictory meaning is attributed in metaphysics. That which it seeks to describe is in fact sub-jected to no one and to no thing: on the contrary, it is the origin of every one and of every thing.

We have been attributing positivity to the negative aspect of duality! How ridiculous we are! Clearly to attribute negativity to its own positive aspect would be equally absurd. Perhaps if we were to bring the two poles together we would short-circuit ourselves? Would that be Satori? Or would it be what we think of as death?

Let the life-current flow from one pole to the other, freely, or rather recognise that such is what takes place in duality— is not that living in accordance with nature, as Lao Tze wished us to do? Is not that living in the present, which we do not? Is not that spontaneity?

If we do that—may not the way lie open for the intuition that in a further dimension the two poles are one, so-called subject and its objects being two aspects of one whole, and that we ourselves are just—reality?

Notes:

A. Subject and object, positive and negative, can have no independent existence; when one appears both are present: therefore they are one whole thing in reality. Are we the obverse or reverse of a coin, the effigy of the sovereign or the symbols of sovereignty, "heads" or "tails," "subject" or "objects"? We are the coin itself—nothing else in the reality of this image; in its dual aspect we *appear* as both sovereign and symbols, but our reality is just gold.

B. As subject I speak, look, listen, as subject I am action—but that which seems to do it is object.

74 ·~ Absolutely Us

Do we remember that the Absolute and the Relative (conditioned) are also a pair of complementaries? It follows that neither can exist independently of the other, and that everything relative is inherently absolute.

A hierarchy of dualities may be convenient for analytical purposes, but it would be unnecessary to suppose that it actually exists.

We may be sure, therefore, that the subject-objects duality which we are is also directly the Absolute and the Relative. And, since the Absolute is divisible infinitely or not at all, each of us is the Absolute absolutely.

The Old Man in the Corner

Professor Suzuki tells us of a Chinese official, resting in his office after his day's work, who awoke to a satori during a thunderstorm and remarked: "And there was the old man in all his homeliness."

Perhaps any image in dualistic language is as good as any other, any description of the indescribable being only a pointing finger, but the homely old man in the corner may be more significant to us than the Buddha-nature, the original face, pure consciousness, or universal mind.

There he sits, the homely old man, always in his corner, hidden by the smoke-screen of thought and phenomena.

75 ⁓ *Objects in Duality Are Not Subjects in Duality*

Several times it has been observed that the object of the subject cannot be itself, i.e. as such, a conscious, dynamic, active agent.

When possible it is comforting to refer to the words of the enlightened who spoke from the awakened state, since what we others say are no better than rumours—except in so far as our words may seek to interpret genuine intuitions. Huang Po, *Wan Ling Record*, N. 42, states, *"Let me repeat that the perceived cannot perceive."*

In so far as we are percepts or concepts, therefore, we can neither perceive nor transform perceptions into concepts. Have we understood—for the fact is vital for our understanding of what we are? That which, all that which, we can perceive or conceive as ourselves, our neighbours, or anything else, is incapable itself of perception or of conception, i.e. *it has no mind of its own.*

Therefore WE are not that objective element, cannot possibly be that—since we say "we," i.e. we are not objects in so far as we are dynamic. . . .

Let us draw our own conclusions, all that results from this information; pointing fingers are not ladders to the moon.

Note: It is the subject of the object that supplies the dynamic characteristics. If we would realise this instead of attributing subjectivity to its object there would be no room left for the activity of an imaginary "ego," which consists precisely in this misplaced attribution.

76 ·~ Existing, Not-Existing or Not Not-Existing? A Somewhat Tedious Discussion

It is generally the practice to seek or assume an Ultimate Unicity beyond every imaginable dualism. But that attempt can never succeed, for every term we choose has its opposite or complementary: even terms such as Tao and Principle of Consciousness can only exist for us in virtue of Non-Tao and Derivative of Consciousness, and "X" in function of "Non-X," just as the useful term "Non-Dual Consciousness" is itself one half of a pair of opposites. "Therefore beware of clinging to one half of a pair" Huang Po warned us.

The process of seeking such a term can never succeed, for it is a cat chasing its own tail or a man pursuing his shadow, the reason being that concepts themselves are dualistic, and therefore the word-symbols that express them.

Surely it is preferable for the cat to accept her tail, and the man his shadow, and for us to state the duality as such in its full formula as Reality-Non-Reality, Absolute-Relative, since the two faces of the coin represent the coin itself? Yet we mean something, that is, we have understood something, every time we seek to express the unicity beyond duality. In using a term such as the Absolute, Reality, Non-Duality, Tao, we wish to express that intuition even if we have to employ a term that only implies half of it.

But are we as stupid as we think we are? Why cannot we say "the Absolute," meaning both Absolute as such and Absolute in its dualistic aspect as the complement of Relative? Words are our servants, not our masters. If I wish to indicate non-duality I use that word to that end, at the same time being perfectly well aware that the term "duality" and that which it represents is inevitably implied in the term "Non-Duality" itself. Yes, but "Non-Duality" just *is not* what I am seeking to express, the Absolute *is not* absolute, for they have duality and the relative tied to their tails!

It cannot be said, for it cannot be thought: it is a will-o-the-wisp. Dualism is with us like a shadow, whichever way we turn, and we are deceiving ourselves when we imagine that there can be for us anything that transcends duality.

This discussion is *not* pointless. Does it not demonstrate that we are deceiving ourselves whenever we imagine that we are talking about non-duality? As far as we are concerned there just is no such thing. It is non-duality that DOES NOT EXIST for us.

Either we exist, and non-duality does not, or it exists, and we do not. Which is it? Where does the weight of evidence lie?

Materialism and positivistic science believe the former; metaphysics and esoteric religion the latter. If it is we who exist, then metaphysics and esoteric religion are just dream-structures; if non-duality (or what we wish to mean by that) exists, then it is we and all we stand for, see and know, that are a dream of the one mind.

It looks as though one can take one's choice. But if one chooses Non-Duality—then, for Heaven's sake, let us hear no more of ourselves and our ego-notions, or anything about us, as though any of that ever was, ever is, or ever will be anything but phantoms of disordered imagination.

"Finally, remember that from first to last not even the smallest grain of anything perceptible (graspable, attainable, tangible) has ever existed or ever will exist." (Huang Po, *Wan Ling Record,* N. 52)

Note: When the sages stated that we should not regard the Absolute etc. as either existing or not-existing, it might be thought that they implied that it could not exist for us, but that it existed for Itself. And when they added that neither should It be regarded as not not-existing they might have been referring to our intuition that something of the kind *ought* to exist, an intuition confirmed by the Awakened.

It is more probable, however, that they implied that the Absolute belongs to a further dimension, to which neither the concept of existing nor that of not-existing is applicable.

77 ·– Reintegrating the Subject

The Masters are continually telling us to cease image-making, conceptualisation, mentation of all kinds, and to rest in the void. As with the abolition of the notion of a so-called "ego" or "self"—every term is employed, so that no loop-hole shall be left. Again and again Huang Po says, "If only you would do that," explicitly stating that it is the only way, and that, in certain cases at least, it will surely open the way for the final and supreme intuition.

What, then, is this so very important process, and this void? The process is surely the original form of Dhyana, so unfortunately translated "Meditation"—how much less inaccurate an idea they would have given us if they had rendered it as "Non-meditation," though "Meditation-Non-meditation" may be a more valid description of it.

No doubt there are people among us who understand this process and who even practise it, but I have never knowingly had the good fortune to meet one of the West, and some people go out to the far-East in order to learn it. Even so one wonders what, in fact, they learn, and, more particularly, if that really is what the Masters meant—since they roundly condemned "meditation." In meditation there is movement; in concentration there is effort; in dhyana there is neither.

The aim is "to destroy the concept-forming dualistic mentality" by means of "wisdom coming from non-dualism," i.e. transcendental (intuitive) knowledge destroys conceptual knowledge, the latter being inevitably erroneous. In short it is dualistic thought which has to be transcended. Later Huang Po goes so far as to say, "Yes, my advice is to give up all indulgence in conceptual thought and intellectual processes. When such things no longer trouble you, you will unfailingly reach Supreme Enlightenment."

Moreover the term "void," even tempered with the assurance that it is also a "plenitude," is highly repugnant, if not terrifying, to most of us, and the idea of letting go of our precious intellect, even for a moment, is almost unbearable.

Suppose we approach the problem, since evidently it is vital and of supreme importance, in our own way and in our own terms, since those of the Masters come down to us via dubious translations (all translations from ancient Chinese pictograms must necessarily be dubious), dating back a thousand years, and of words spoken by and to men of a different race and a very different culture from our own.

Is the answer not simple—as answers should be, if they are real? Are the Masters not asking us just to withdraw our subjectivity from the object, thereby reintegrating the subject?

Is that not something we can understand? Is that not something we can do? And when we do that are we not invulnerable? Was it not from that state Socrates said, "Ils peuvent me tuer, mais ils ne peuvent pas me faire de mal"?

In that state, if someone comes and insults us, practises a fraud upon us, or strikes us—we do not react. How could we? What we misinterpreted as an "ego" is no longer there. It is almost as though we were reading about such actions in a newspaper, only, in the latter case, we tend to identify ourselves with the victim—and react.

In that state the mind is still, but there is no lack of, but increased awareness. It is a state of *disponibilité*. No concepts arise, but intuition can enter freely. Its tranquillity is restorative, and its serenity has an element of bliss.

The Maharshi seems to have been in that state when his ashram was attacked by robbers. And did not Ouspensky seek to inculcate a similar practice, which I think he called "self-remembering"? Thank Goodness there is nothing original in what I suggest! I hope indeed there never is, else how could such suggestion be valid?

Reintegrate the subject, then the object and all objects will be just such and no more. Surely that is life in dualism as it should be lived in dualism, and the life of man as it was before the "Fall"? Surely that state is the famous "void"—and there is no "ego," or anything to be mistaken for that, anywhere in existence.

PHYSICS AND METAPHYSICS

78 ·- Sense and Non-Sense

TOM: I must be very stupid.
DICK: Not unlikely, but what evidence have you?
TOM: I understand nothing!
DICK: That is a sign of intelligence, not of stupidity.
TOM: Glad to hear it.
DICK: Only the stupid can suppose that they understand.
TOM: Yet we all want to.
HARRY: Not at all: I haven't the slightest desire.

TOM: Why does he think like that?

DICK: People who accept without question that appearances are real or, as we should put it, who mistake phenomena for reality, see no problem.

HARRY: None of the kind you argue about anyhow.

TOM: Don't they ever suspect anything, ever smell a rat?

DICK: Of course they do. Why do you think they spend their lives running away from themselves as fast as their legs and their wheels and their bars-and-cafes can carry them?

HARRY: Tcheuh! We enjoy life: you don't!

DICK: Superficially that is true enough: we seek something beyond enjoyment, for we know that is only one part of a whole, and that the counterpart cannot be avoided.

TOM: When they do face up to the question they see that life is inexplicable and that nothing makes sense. But they get no further.

DICK: An increasing number do get further, but they get stuck in the mud because there are no qualified teachers in the West. An understanding that the visible world is phenomenal and that noumenon, or reality, is an invisible cause, is not sufficient. Conditioning is too strong.

TOM: They are unable to believe what the Masters tell them?

DICK: Intellectually they may believe, but habit is hard to overcome. They continue to think and act as though they and everything around them were real and all the reality there is.

HARRY: Nearly everything you say is just crazy nonsense to us. It is as though you took every normal and evident fact and substituted a long-winded absurdity for it.

We can hardly believe our ears, or imagine how any apparently sane persons can seriously talk such rubbish.

TOM: Crude, but perhaps good for us to hear?

DICK: Harmless and inoffensive; moreover Harry has a shrewd suspicion that it is not so, haven't you, Harry?

HARRY: Well, the rot you talk rings a bell now and again, though it rarely makes sense.

DICK: What in particular is it you don't understand, Tom? Who knows, I might have a clue.

TOM: This subject-object business. When the object speaks with the maximum of false identification and absurdity, as, for instance, every time Harry opens his mouth, who is in fact speaking?

DICK: The subject, of course. Who else is there to speak?

TOM: Even when the object speaks one hundred per cent as object.

DICK: Even then.

TOM: But how is that? How can it be?

DICK: Subject can use an object to speak as subject—as when Maharshi spoke, or, under identification, subject can speak as object under that absurd limitation—as when Harry speaks, or you and I when someone treads on our toe.

TOM: So that the withdrawal of subjectivity from the object means. . . .

DICK: Just that. Exactly what it says.

TOM: And reintegration in the subject. . . .

DICK: That is the same adjustment. Subject uses an object as before as a mechanism of dualistic expression, but *via*, not *as*, the object employed.

TOM: Yet subject and object are one?

DICK: Subject and all objects are one in reality, but in

dualistic manifestation they are apparently separate—like the obverse and reverse of a coin, each of which has a different appearance, representing to you the reality of the coin itself which you cannot see.

TOM: But what puzzles me is that subject might speak via Harry instead of via you or me, at any moment, since we are all objects.

DICK: Subject not only might but does.

HARRY: With this difference, that when the blighter speaks via me he talks sense for a change. Why is that now?

DICK: When he talks sense subject is "speaking" as an object; when he talks metaphysics, real nonsensical metaphysics to you, he may be "speaking" as subject.

HARRY: How do you know?

DICK: Only chaps like you are in the happy position of knowing things. We, poor lunatics, are inclined to believe that when knowledge comes in the form of intuition, that is, in a flash, it is probably direct from the subject; otherwise it comes, also from the subject but via the intellectual mechanism which objects provide.

HARRY: And in the latter case what makes the difference between the high-falutin twaddle he lets off through you, and the simple common-sense that issues from me?

DICK: If we are identified with ourselves as objects the only difference lies in the composition, make-and-shape of our intellectual apparatus; if we are not so identified, then our thought is not distorted by the I-notion as yours is.

HARRY: A regular polyglot, that subject fellow, isn't he?

TOM: What do you mean?

HARRY: He comes through in English, French, German,

Chinese, Hindustani, any old lingo that happens to be required.

DICK: "He" comes through, as you put it so well, but not in any lingo.

HARRY: What do you mean?

DICK: "He" does not speak.

HARRY: Does not speak? But his speaking is the subject of this crazy conversation! I give it up, or rather I withdraw, and reintegrate my own skin!

DICK: The subject is not a "person," and it does not speak. It is the object, the psycho-somatic apparatus, that speaks. The subject informs that which is expressed, if you will.

HARRY: What is it then? A ghost?

DICK: Not even that. Much less material.

HARRY: What can be less material than a ghost?

DICK: Something that is formless, impersonal, imperceptible, and outside time.

HARRY: Sounds like a description of nothing.

DICK: Exactly. It is, as you say, no thing.

TOM: Just a concept?

DICK: Just.

TOM: And therefore unreal?

DICK: Quite.

TOM: And inexistent?

DICK: Surely

HARRY: Goodbye, goodbye, I'm off—in case they take me to the loony-bin also. . . .

TOM: Too much for Harry! He will never understand anything.

DICK: There have been greater miracles.

TOM: You said just now that the two sides of a coin represent its reality which we cannot see. How do they do that?

DICK: You can only see the obverse and the reverse, and never at once, the appearance called "coin," because they are unreal projects: you cannot see the reality, the suchness, though you have a concept for it called "gold."

TOM: If we did not see the appearance, heads and tails, see the one and imagine the other, there would be no object?

DICK: None.

TOM: But when we see the appearance there is "behind" it a suchness which we cannot see?

DICK: The relative reality is what you call "gold" but that is only a concept: its suchness is not a shape, or a weight, or anything sensorially perceptible.

TOM: Not even a vibration, or rate of vibration?

DICK: I do not think so. A vibration is merely a vaguer and more subtle concept. The suchness you seek to imagine, but never can, is of another order altogether, of an order that is of no order.

TOM: Something that has existence in a further dimension?

DICK: I see no objection to the image.

REALITY AND MANIFESTATION

79 ⸱– *The Dharma*

TWO: In your opinion, what *is* the *Dharma?*

ONE: If you are looking for the Buddha—try the opposite direction. No, not there . . . Nor there . . . Nor there either.

TWO: Where then?

ONE: Not outside—*inside!*

TWO: Ass! Now you can answer my question.

ONE: Do you remember how the Zen Masters replied to such questions?

TWO: Held up their walking-stick, pointed to a tree or a pillar, or gave you a good kick in the pants.

ONE: Quite so.

TWO: We are not in ninth-century China; answer like a Christian.

ONE: The Gnostic scriptures of esoteric Christianity were burnt by the Gothic Fathers of the Church, whereby the re-ligion taught by Jesus Himself rapidly came to an end.

TWO: Rapidly? Do not traces still remain?

ONE: Traces, yes. But I might get Padma Sambhava to answer you in Tibetan.

TWO: Good enough. Attaboy! But you needn't say everything twenty times over; even so it'll be long enough!

ONE: Quite. First statement:
"Inasmuch as from eternity there is nothing whatsoever to be practised, there is no need to fall under the sway of erroneous methods."

TWO: Fine! Straight from the shoulder! That lets out almost everyone I know; they are all busy on doctrines and methods, systems, disciplines and what have you.

ONE: The temptation is too strong, but unfortunately by yielding to it they strengthen the very notion of which they are trying to rid themselves. The second statement:
"The non-created, self-radiant Wisdom here set forth . . . is itself the perfect practice."

TWO: Good. And promising. Which is? . . .

ONE: Patience, here it is. Third statement:
         "There being no two such things as action and per-
         former of action, if one seeks the performer of action
         and no performer of action be found anywhere,
         thereupon the goal of all fruit-obtaining is reached
         and also the final consummation itself."

TWO: Admirable! That is to say, the only performer of
         action is action itself. But why does he need about
         forty words to say that when nine would suffice?

ONE: An English author would have needed a hundred
         and fifty thousand.

TWO: A book? You have taught me to prefer living nour-
         ishment that I can digest for myself.

ONE: Nevertheless if a bullet were small enough it would
         leave no trace. But the English word "action" lacks an
         important precision, it can imply either that which is
         done, or the doing of it.

TWO: Are they not one?

ONE: In duality—no. The "doing of it" is subjective and
         relatively real; "that which is done" is objective and
         illusory.

TWO: And the former is what is meant?

ONE: Just as it is the realisation that is dynamic, rather
         than that which is realised. Fourth statement:
         "There being no method whatsoever of obtaining
         the fruit, there is no need to fall under the sway of
         the dualities of accepting or rejecting this teaching."

TWO: Clear and concise! Go on—it is fine. . . .

ONE: That is the end; there is no more to be said.

TWO: That is . . . all?

ONE: What more could be needed? Does it not say every-
         thing?

TWO: If one is ready—yes, perhaps.

ONE: We are so used to overeating . . . I can add his colophon if you like?

TWO: I'd like to hear that.

ONE: "Thereupon is attained the goal of the seeking, and also the end of the search itself. Then nothing more is there to be sought; nor is there need to seek anything."

TWO: The same graceful charm and finality.

ONE: Are you satisfied?

TWO: You are right. I see that it should be enough. Indeed it *is* the Dharma. You have given me what I asked for.

ONE: Go for a walk, and let us hope you will come back awakened.

TWO: Perhaps that will be nearer, if any such event exists at all. But the fruit-bearing will be in its own good time, not in yours or mine.

ONE: The fruit-bearing is not in time. You have only to open your eyes.

TWO: No two things . . . action and performer of action . . . If one seeks . . . and no performer of action to be found anywhere . . . no . . . performer . . . anywhere . . . just action itself . . . Ha, ha, ha!

ONE: I wonder . . . Can he have understood? . . .

PHYSICS AND METAPHYSICS
80 ·- Hard Words

Evasion

Art, literature, music, ornithology, entomology, biology, philosophy, physics, politics. . . .

Value as dualistic activities? Yes? No?

In relative reality, in any case, evasions, one and all, men and women chasing their shadows. And metaphysics? Methods, techniques, disciplines, of whatever sort or kind?

Reality, in its relative aspect, only knows one activity, one question to be answered, and that is "Who?" And one method, which is to look in the right direction.

Note: Any mental activity that is based on the assumption, tacit or admitted, that the thinker is an entity in his own right, is an evasion.

These activities, recognised here as "evasions" of the real problem, could also be misdirected attempts at reintegration with unicity.

REALITY AND MANIFESTATION
81 ⟿ Metaphysical Analysis of What We Are

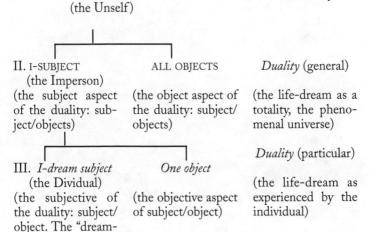

I.   I-REALITY   *Non-duality*
        (the Unself)

II. I-SUBJECT   ALL OBJECTS   *Duality* (general)
    (the Imperson)
(the subject aspect   (the object aspect of   (the life-dream as a
of the duality: sub-   the duality: subject/   totality, the pheno-
ject/objects)   objects)   menal universe)

                                                  Duality (particular)

III. *I-dream subject*   *One object*
    (the Dividual)   (the life-dream as
(the subjective of   (the objective aspect   experienced by the
the duality: subject/   of subject/object)   individual)
object. The "dream-
ed" subject.

Notes:

a)   I-subject am called "The Witness" in Vedanta Advaita.
       I-subject am directly operative in *dhyana* (*ch'an, zen)* from
       which all intellectual activity is excluded.
       I-subject am directly operative in that which Ouspensky
       termed "self-remembering."
       I-subject am the Dreamer of my "life-dream," the "Father."

b)   I-dream-subject am a limited aspect of me as I-subject.
       I-subject am a limited aspect of me as I-reality.

c)   "III" can be regarded as "within" "II," and "II" as "within" "I."

d)   I-dream-subject and my object are me as I-subject.
       I-subject and my objects are ME as I-Reality.
       No object is ever me as object—for I am subject/object.

I-dream-subject and I-subject are one with ME as I-Reality.

e) "We" can be substituted for "I" without in any way affecting the meaning of the analysis; Reality being One—"we" are "I."

f) The term "dream" is used to imply that which is only a concept in consciousness.

g) The ego-notion is just *subjectivity* of the dream-subject erroneously applied to the *object*.

h) The positive, dynamic element of subject/object is subject only.

82 ·- A Trilogy

I. Resolving Our Personal Duality - I

Regarding object as subject is the state of mistaken identification in which we all live, commonly referred to as egoism or belief in our identity with the visible "self."

Ridding ourselves of this false identification by withdrawing subjectivity from the object and so reintegrating the subject, we are liable to find ourselves identified with the subject only *in a manner* which looks upon the object as a thing apart, as a concept that is not us.

This displaced and still partial identification leaves us tied down to the immediate duality of subject/object which inhibits our release.

Having rid ourselves of the false identification with the object, we then need to "reabsorb" the object itself, so that object and subject re-become one.

II. The Process of Release

If I-dream subject infuse and re-absorb my object so that

my object is reintegrated in me, I-dream subject, we thereby re-become one. At that moment we are *I-Subject* itself and *All Objects* that is relative Reality or the dual aspect of I-Reality (the Absolute, Pure Consciousness or Godhead)—which is Enlightenment.

"A perception . . . that subject and object are one . . . by this understanding will you awake to the truth of Zen," i.e. Liberation. (Huang Po, *Wan Ling Record,* 26)

III. Infusion

In what consists this process of "re-absorption" of the object?

Far from seeking to annihilate it as something extraneous to ourselves, the process may appear to us as one of *infusion,* which implies a taking possession of the object by flooding it with the relative reality of the I-subject (the "Father" in the graceful terminology of Jesus).

As an image may we not compare this process to the introduction of a light into a dark room, which dissipates the darkness entirely and may be said to "take possession" of that room? Since the object, being essentially "void," may be described as being composed of "darkness"—nothing then remains but light, which is the "substance" of subject; and so they are one.

Light is an image, but *karuna, caritas,* impersonal love, is a description of the thing itself.

Note 1: It is clear that the unification of object and subject cannot be effected by any action on the part of the subject of that object, but can only arise as a result of action from "above," i.e. on the part of the I-subject which is itself that unification.

Let us not forget that the object, at the same time that it is the object of its subject, is also one of the objects of I-subject, which together constitute the totality of phenomena.

Note 2: The apparent complication of these attempts to envisage that which we are, may be compared to a draughtsman's efforts to represent on a plane-surface and by means of false perspective that which he sees in three dimensions.

What we are exists in what we can only envisage as multiple dimensions, and we have to represent it to ourselves in the three to which we are confined by our perceptions and the language in which we seek to describe them.

If we understand that, we are no longer surprised that something represented as in succession may be at the same time simultaneous in one or more of its aspects. For instance, the first and the last words of this note are separated on the two-dimensional plane-surface on which they are written, but the multidimensional aspect of this page may be represented by bending it over so that its corners meet: in the resulting dimension the first and the last words will appear together or simultaneously. Otherwise one can say that there is no reality in the conception of succession.

Thus no aspect of reality is really separated from any other: it is our attempt to envisage them that obliges us to represent them as separated in time and in space.

PHYSICS AND METAPHYSICS

83 ·- The Reason Why - I

I wonder how much of our trouble may be due to misunderstanding of oriental scriptures ambiguously translated? A translator is not necessarily, indeed perhaps not often, a man who fully understands that which he is translating, and if he understands it intellectually, does that imply that he understands it intuitively? But the oriental scriptures with which we are concerned were composed in order to stimulate intuition rather than to satisfy the intellect, for the former alone is capable of leading to the desired result. In the West, however, we have all been educated to cultivate and rely upon the intellect alone, and to ignore and distrust intuition, closing our eyes to the evident fact that approximately every discovery made by man has been due ultimately to intuition and could never have been made solely by intellect.

The Reason Why - II

Perhaps the outstanding example of one of our major troubles being due to misunderstanding of the oriental scriptures is our widespread attempt to apply literally the exhortation to achieve Detachment and to abandon Discrimination. But these are effects, not causes. Attachment and Discrimination are direct manifestations of the *emprise* of the ego-notion.

People in the West settle down to a determined effort to feel detached, and, by exercise of the so-called will, to avoid discrimination. The effect of this should be obvious: such a proceeding inevitably strengthens the ego-notion which makes the effort. But it is the elimination of the ego-notion that is the primary aim of all the teachings, and things are not eliminated by being strengthened!

Detachment and the abandonment of Discrimination are the inevitable and automatic result of the elimination of an ego-notion, and cannot be brought about by any other means.

We have been doing what primitive medicine did—attacking the symptoms in order to cure a disease, and aggravating the disease by so doing. For instance, a fever is a defensive measure on the part of the body controlled by organic consciousness, and where, by artificial and violent means, doctors counteracted the fever they thereby thwarted the body's defensive mechanism and aggravated the malady.

Need we be surprised at the unsatisfactory results of our efforts? Did the Masters not warn us not to make them?

We have only to eliminate the ego-notion by succeeding in the difficult task of understanding that it does not exist except as a notion. Which, by the way, is the subject/object of this book!

REALITY AND MANIFESTATION

84 ⸗ Awakening by Means of the Dream Can Only Be Dreaming that We Are Awake

Understanding can be approached from "above" or from "below," that is, *via* the I-subject direct or *via* the me-object, *from* the non-dual or *via* duality.

The approaches via the subject are based on the Diamond Sutra, Advaita, the Ch'an of the T'ang Masters, or the teaching of Padma Sambhava. All these are brief and concise, and were in general regarded as "secret" doctrines because accessible only to the few who were capable of understanding at that level, also perhaps because they would necessarily appear meaningless and even absurd to the simple-minded. All the other approaches of which I have cognisance are via the object. How could they possibly succeed? What could they achieve beyond a conditioning of the psyche?

To seek to dispose of an illusory object by means of itself is surely a sheer impossibility.

Note: "I" alone am the subject. "That which does" is an object. "I" is ultimately pure unconditioned Subject, non-dual; subject conditioned by object is dual. (The term "unconditioned subject," as such, is self-contradictory, but it is used to imply subject and object united in a unicity that cannot be given any possible name.)

WORK AND PLAY

85 ·- *The Criminal - I*

TWO: You said just now that nothing can be either right or wrong for me in itself, since no action can comport what is only a relative estimation. Do you mean that to apply to criminal acts also?

ONE: Criminal acts? What are they?

TWO: Acts punishable by law.

ONE: The legal fiction that any specific act is in itself a "crime," regardless of the circumstances in which it was committed, makes nonsense, regarded metaphysically. The act is an act, and nothing else whatever. The qualities projected upon it are points on a scale of relative values, and quite unreal.

TWO: But surely some acts are mischievous and others anodyne?

ONE: Acts may be estimated as base or admirable, or anything in between, according to the code of values that happens to be fashionable in a given community at a given moment.

TWO: Still, they must be codified somehow?

ONE: Is that so? In countries such as England—and there may be others—in which man tends to be regarded as made for laws, rather than laws for man, laws are applied practically regardless of circumstances, and the degree of injustice that results has to be seen to be believed. Strange to say, it is not seen, by most people, so hypnotised are they by the sacrosanctity of "laws" as things-in-themselves, and by moral prig-gishness.

TWO: But should not laws have what you term "sacrosanc-tity?"

ONE: Nothing should have what it cannot possess.

TWO: So it is the circumstances governing an act, rather than the act itself, that really matter?

ONE: By what other means could an act be understood, and, by understanding, judged—if it should be nec-essary to judge it at all?

TWO: But do not current passions, eulogistically called "public opinion," influence the administration of jus-tice less in England than in countries such as France?

ONE: It would seem to be so, but what is termed "justice" is itself a legal fiction.

TWO: That, however, applies to every country.

ONE: Every country. And the ludicrous spectacle of human beings solemnly, even piously, sitting in judgment on their own enemies, and taking vengeance on them, after wars and upheavals, called "punishment," with an elaborate show of formalities, has become current practice the world over. The distribution of bouquets to any country, least of all the one into which one happens to have been born, is quite unjustified.

TWO: Do you mean that I can commit murder without being thereby necessarily a criminal?

ONE: In the eyes of the "law"—no; in the eyes of the eter-nal—of course.

TWO: Give me an example.

ONE: Unnecessary, think for yourself. To kill a man, in cer-tain circumstances, may be perfectly justifiable; to kill a pigeon, in other circumstances, may be perfect-ly unjustifiable. But you will be hung for the former

122

and praised for the latter, whereas you ought to be hung for the latter and praised for the former.

TWO: But, after all, a pigeon is only a pigeon!

ONE: And a man is only a man.

TWO: Still, there is a difference!

ONE: If so, I don't know it.

TWO: Man is infinitely superior!

ONE: In what?

TWO: In . . . in ability.

ONE: Yes, he kills better.

TWO: He does everything better.

ONE: Nonsense. Dogs smell better. Hawks see better. Bats hear better. Horses run faster. Birds fly better. Insects work better. All animals know better. Man has only one clear superiority.

TWO: Which is?

ONE: As a beast of prey he is supreme. In the Last Judgment, before Moloch, the lion will hang his head, the vulture will turn away, the jackal will put his tail between his legs, when man appears, his hands dripping with the blood of his fellow creatures, clad in their skins, their bones rattling in his ears, and their flesh rotting in his guts. Whereas the score of the other beasts of prey will be counted in digits, his will be counted in hecatombs. Moloch himself will bow before him in admiration.

TWO: But still . . . but still. . . .

ONE: But still man is just part of nature, one small part, one of many creatures, and no one gave him special rights to torture and slaughter the others at his good pleasure, which he does on account of the cunning which he derives from his faculty of turning percepts into concepts on a scale which in the others is either instinctive or rudimentary.

TWO: A terrible requisition indeed!

ONE: Would any of the world's prophets or sages dispute it?

TWO: I cannot say that they would. But man justifies himself in his own eyes.

ONE: One of England's most famous criminal lawyers stated, towards the end of his life, that he had never defended a criminal who did not believe himself to be innocent.

TWO: Nevertheless don't you think that man's self-justifications should be considered?

ONE: By all means. What are they?

TWO: They are probably legion, from religion to commercial necessity.

ONE: A religion that authorises man to torture and slaughter and exploit his fellow-creatures is quite unworthy of consideration as religion. It could only be an ethic devised by men for the unrestrained exploitation of the ego-complex. That is not a religion at all, and nothing of the kind was either explicit or implicit in the teachings of Sri Krishna, the Buddha, or Jesus, but precisely the opposite of that.

TWO: Religions are apt to be turned upside down, and to become ethics only, in the hands of later generations who have never understood the teachings of the founder.

ONE: Quite so, but then they are no longer religions except in name. The re-ligion—re-uniting (with God)— may survive in certain aspects of each sect or church, but an ethic, even a good one, is not a religion.

TWO: There should be other justifications.

ONE: There can be no justification for becoming an enemy

of that to which you belong, that of which you form a part; and man forms a part of nature. Ignorance may be an excuse, probably the best, but it is not a justification.

TWO: And commercial necessity?

ONE: Whatever could that be? There is quite certainly no such thing. The word "necessity" is entirely inapplicable to such an activity as commerce. Commerce is merely the organisation of greed, of avidity, of grasping, unless it places service to the community before personal gain. When it does that it fulfills a useful, but never a necessary, function; when it does not, it constitutes an unmitigated evil alike to those who exploit it and to the public that suffers from it.

TWO: And to which category does modern commerce as at present observable belong?

ONE: Look about you—and stop asking me questions you can answer yourself!

TWO: But is there no punishment for enmity to nature?

ONE: If you mean vengeance—who is there to avenge?

TWO: "Vengeance is mine, saith the Lord, I will repay."

ONE: Any such Lord must be on a par with those on whom he wreaks vengeance. Do you know of one? To the only Power that is Real such a word would have no meaning whatever.

TWO: Penalty then.

ONE: Of course there is a penalty. No one can exploit nature without paying a penalty. But it is not recognizable in the context of our absurd and primary notions of punishment and vengeance.

TWO: What is it then?

ONE: It is an impartial, impersonal process that appears to us as cause and effect. But we hardly notice its workings, for it does not trouble to wear a wig and a gown.

TWO: Then how do we know it?

ONE: In the West I doubt if many of us do. In the East it is known as *karma*. Unfortunately that word also has suffered at the hands of people who do not understand it, but it connotes a tremendous reality.

TWO: Does every man who exploits nature, regards nature as his enemy, or persecutes his fellow-creatures suffer equally?

ONE: I regard that as unlikely. You yourself can observe at any time that a price must be paid for the exploitation of nature. That has even been enshrined in popular wisdom: "Tout se paye"—as any French peasant will tell you. Even the price can often be observed, if you look closely enough and have a sane sense of values.

TWO: But where individuals are concerned?

ONE: Less easy to follow—for the penalty is not paid to a policeman on the spot as for minor motoring offences in France. And it seems likely that you who understand would pay more heavily than a man who persecuted his fellow-creatures in complete ignorance and failure to realise that they are such, regarding himself as some kind of deity specially authorised by the Almighty to injure everybody but himself.

TWO: But he would pay a penalty nevertheless?

ONE: Undoubtedly. If it did nothing else his action would be added to the weight of ignorance on his shoulders, and would still further impede his prospects of rising out of darkness and misery into the light of understanding.

TWO: But surely the world around us today, a prey to envy, hatred and malice, greed, violence, and fraud, with governments as greedy and dishonest as any of those they misrule, is the clearest evidence of this process of cause and effect, which in the East is called *karma*?

ONE: You have answered your own question more conclusively than I was able to answer it, and more simply.

TWO: Ignorance and misery in the spirit, amidst material prosperity, pseudo prosperity; topsy-turvy, pseudo freedom, pseudo justice—that is the price, the penalty. And anxiety. Can it be remedied?

ONE: Every action comports within itself a reaction, materialism *à l'outrance* like any other excess. Observe the upsurge, the thirst for what are regarded as "spiritual" doctrines.

TWO: Can that ever get the upper hand?

ONE: We are not prophets. But nature will recover her own. She does not use clocks. Just consider: were the disproportionate numbers of the human species on this Earth to be readjusted, what might we expect?

TWO: In what direction?

ONE: If the population were reduced tenfold would not the incitements to envy, hatred and malice, greed, anger, violence, etc., be reduced a hundredfold? Would not nature reassert herself? Would not most of the pseudo problems dissolve into thin air? Would not mankind once more live in harmony with nature?

TWO: Hierarchies might arise, and rule by individuals.

ONE: That is not contrary to the laws of nature.

TWO: But could it happen? Will it happen?

ONE: Everything can happen. Everything will happen.

TWO: Some time or other?

ONE: For in the dream of the One Mind everything is.

TWO: And that uses no clocks!

86 ·– The Criminal – II

TWO: I am not satisfied about our chat yesterday: the criminal and all that.

ONE: Good. But we are unable to talk on two levels at the same time.

TWO: Padma Sambhava revealed to us that we could not find a performer of an action, and that the discovery of that opens the way to full comprehension.

ONE: If your intuition verifies that—it is so.

TWO: Therefore there is no criminal.

ONE: He is only a concept.

TWO: But you seemed to imply that the circumstances of the "crime" were all that mattered.

ONE: Well?

TWO: We understood that it is not an action itself that is real, but the doing of it, not that which is realised or done, but the realising.

ONE: Undoubtedly.

TWO: So the "crime" is not real either, but just the act of perpetration?

ONE: The doer is a concept, the deed is a concept, the doing is real.

TWO: Since there is no criminal and no crime, but only a doing—what is there to judge?

ONE: If there had been a recording of our conversation I think you would find that it was implicit that there was nothing to judge.

TWO: But why should the circumstances of an unreal

action committed by nobody have any importance?

ONE: You are trying to talk on two levels simultaneously. Such an acrobatic manipulation of language is nearly impossible. The law is an artificial structure of imagination, gratuitously associated with the idea of "justice," that attempts to suppress the results of acts that are only concepts, performed by individuals that are not such, in a context controlled by cause-and-effect.

TWO: But why, then, do the circumstances matter?

ONE: The circumstances you refer to are the cause-and-effect as a result of which the apparent action occurs.

TWO: So there is reality in that?

ONE: Cause-and-effect are what we have referred to as *karma*. Those who have fully understood, who are awake, who no longer mistake themselves for the object of a dream-subject, and who have realised that they are in the world of appearances dream-subject and its objects undivided, that is, who can know themselves as I-subject when they will, are no longer victims of *karma*. But the rest of us, and even the awakened as long as life lasts, being subject to our psycho-somatic apparatus while living our dream, remain apparently in this world of appearances, and have to play our part therein.

TWO: Like actors in a play?

ONE: The image is the Maharshi's, and good. That life is purely phenomenal but it appears to be real, as our own dream-life does. And we can, indeed we have to, regard it as such, and speak of it as such in daily conversation. Otherwise we should be cut off from our fellow-men.

TWO: So the action, the "crime" when the action is so regarded, is just a result of cause-and-effect, of *karma* if you will, and the punishment inflicted by the law is that also, the circumstances being *karma* also, the result of cause-and-effect, and the punishment inflicted on the dream-subject/object part of the same process although imagined to be a vengeance or a deterrent applied to a perfectly free and independent individual?

ONE: I thoroughly agree with your interpretation. It may be difficult to express it more succinctly.

TWO: I wonder, is it worth discussing these matters at all!

ONE: The Maharshi, since we have just mentioned him, probably did not think so. He only spoke when people insisted. His kindness was ubiquitous and unlimited.

TWO: Then we should not blame man for his outrageous attitude towards that nature of which he is himself an integral part?

ONE: We should not blame anyone for anything. Who is there to blame?

TWO: But still . . . but still. . . .

ONE: You want to blame man for not understanding what he is, that he is not what he thinks, that poor, poor thing, but something unimaginably superior. But blame is not the word.

TWO: Pity perhaps?

ONE: Provided no element of contempt lies therein.

TWO: What remains of "pity" is then pure *karuna-caritas?*

ONE: Which is understanding itself.

TWO: But how can he be brought to understand?

ONE: He cannot. Only he, as I-subject, can do that.

TWO: And that?

ONE: By following his urge, the urge that every dream-subject/object has, for that is his link with Reality.

87 · Street Scene

Being infatuated by sense objects, and thereby shutting themselves from their own light, all sentient beings, tormented by outer circumstances and inner vexations, act voluntarily as slaves to their own desires . . . they are kind in words, but wicked in mind; they are greedy, malignant, jealous, crooked, flattering, egotistic, offensive to men and destructive to inanimate objects . . . should they rectify their heart, so that wisdom arises perpetually, the mind would be under introspection, and evil-doing be replaced by the practice of good. . . .

WEI LANG, 69-70

We noticed something of the kind the other day. Let's do something about it. Or can we? Could he?

Tinkle-Tinkle

People running away from themselves as fast as wheels can take them, always hoping they have left themselves behind, putting their feet more firmly on the accelerator every time they perceive that they are still there, like animals with a tin can tied to their tails. Neither ever seems to stop and try to find out what is there; if they did they would realise that it is only a tin can, quite empty—or void as the Buddhists like to describe it.

REALITY AND MANIFESTATION

88 ·~ Resolving Our Personal Duality - II

It is not possible to reunite colours separated by a prism, nor is it possible to reunite object and subject, on the plane on which they appear as such. In order to "see" them reunited it is necessary to perceive them as they were before they were separated by the prism, for the prism holds them apart. Behind the prism red and green appear reunited as white, and object and subject reunited as "I."

A perception that subject and object are one—as Huang Po told us, resulting in Liberation—cannot be a perception on the part of the objects of that perception. The act of perception, more precisely the perceiving, must be "transferred" from the dream-subject to the I-subject. More precisely, since the dream-subject is merely such as such, and all perceptions derive from I-subject, even when they are perceived dualistically via the dream-subject, this vital, indeed capital, act of perception, which is just a perceiving, must be a *direct* perceiving on the part of I-subject, in which the dream-subject and object are seen as one. As long as the perceiving appears as a perception on the part of a dream-subject/object this can never be.

Expressed dimensionally, an act of perception in the three dimensions of dream-life cannot "see" the duality of subject and object as one; the perceiving must take place in the further dimension in which that duality actually is, and must always be, one. The perceiving itself is not different, for there are not multiple kinds of perception, but it is a pure, that is, a direct, perceiving.

To suppose that such perceiving is unobtainable, is even essentially difficult, is surely a delusion and an effect of erroneous identification, of seeing by what we imagine to be an "ego." That delusion removed, dissolved, short-circuited, transcended, the perceiving itself rebecomes normal and direct, and I-dream subject/object should readily be perceived as one. We then have only to open our eyes and perceive it if we will—since we are the I-subject that perceives.

Note 1: Since subject cannot perceive itself, we saw this process the other day as Infusion, as *karuna-caritas* envisaged as light, and that may be a helpful stage in the process of understanding, but that is also *prajna,* pure wisdom, for they are two aspects of one "thing," *buddhi* perhaps—since we find it necessary to label each apparent element of our discrete understanding in order to conceive it. But the sooner the labels are torn off and burnt the better, and the nearer we are to understanding itself. Let us now scrap the lot and jump to the comprehension that these "things" are just analytical devices for describing the process of perceiving itself. That perceiving may be "seen" or "felt" as *prajna,* as *karuna,* be labelled as *buddhi,* or envisaged as light, but they do not exist in their own right as anything, even as the stuff or plenitude of the "Void." It is the perceiving, the movement in consciousness itself, that thereby "fuses" object and subject so that their unity is re-established as "I."

Note 2: In "Resolving Our Personal Duality—1" we saw this process, described as "infusion," in an apparent time-sequence in which the infusion seemed to be the "cause" of the reintegration of object in subject. But, regarded in a time-sequence, it may be better seen as a "result" of reintegration, as the cognition that follows or accompanies such integration.

In fact, however, it should be the integrating itself, or, if one prefers, the perception of that integration, in other words the perceiving of perceiving.

PHYSICS AND METAPHYSICS

89 ·— Geometrical Representation of Our Multidimensional Reality

In order to represent our metaphysical reality we are obliged to imitate the draughtsman who presents, on a two-dimensional plane surface, that which he perceives in three dimensions, by means of a device known as false perspective. This necessity is imposed upon us because we have no way in which we can either conceive or represent any further dimension except by means of mathematical formulae.

Let us regard total reality as an infinite sphere, and let us make a model of it, of finite and practical dimensions. Take a transparent globe and pass it through a slicing machine, thereby reducing it to the greatest possible number of transparent rings of negligible thickness, each one representing two dimensions only. Each of these represents the individual subject/object, the inner surface representing the subject-aspect, the outer surface the object aspect. When we reconstitute the globe and place it on the level of our eyes, each of the superimposed rings of two dimensions, visible or not as individual rings, represent what I have been calling I-dream subject/object. Then let us regard the globe from "above." From that angle the rings, seen in what we may colloquially describe as "thickness," i.e. in a further dimension, represent the relative subject/objects, which I have been calling I-subject/objects. It will be observed that the rings are of decreasing diameter as they approach the "poles," until there-at they have one dimension only. That which appears as one-dimensional at the poles increases towards the centre of the globe, and constitutes the entire within of the structure. That represents a further dimension, and is I-Reality itself.

Seen from the poles, three-dimensionally, the individual rings no longer exist as such—they, I-dream subject/object—are merged in the totality of rings, which represent I-subject/objects. But at the poles that totality appears as one, I-subject having merged in its centre (which, in this image, has to appear as an axis). But that centre, viewed as an axis but not really such, spreads out in all directions within the globe, and is in direct contact with all parts of it. Not only is it in direct contact with all parts of the globe, but it is inevitably itself all parts of it—so that, in effect, the globe no longer has any parts. That is, from within it is one whole, whereas viewed from without it appears to be composed of a solid mass of rings, or of individual rings, according to the dimension from which it is viewed.

This representation may enable us to envisage Reality as the totality it must be, in direct contact with every part of itself, also its relative aspect, I-subject/objects, as a solid surface or sheath (expanding to infinity), and, from yet another angle, each individual ring, representing our conceptual existence, composing that sheath. From each further view-point or dimension the lesser one appears as a unity, although it has an inner and an outer side which represents its aspect as subject and as object.

I do not know if it may be possible more accurately to represent visually our multidimensional reality.

90 — The Term "Enlightenment"

It is quite evident that the Chinese pictogram translated as "enlightenment" has two different meanings.

For instance, when the Buddha's enlightenment is referred to it is usually described as "complete and perfect

Enlightenment." Therefore we know that "incomplete" and "imperfect" enlightenment must have been recognised.

In the Sutra of Wei Lang, on the other hand, "enlightenment" occurs to whole audiences at the end of a discourse, and to individuals as a result of the elucidation of minor problems.

I have heard it maintained that both cases are just examples of oriental hyperbole. That this is not so is proved by Section 20 of the *Chün Chou Record* of Huang Po, wherein the term is used three times to denote cases of enlightenment "from without," of an evidently different, or at most partial, nature, and three times to describe cases of enlightenment "from within the subject's own mind" or "through the Dharma of Mind."

If further proof were needed, Section 55 of the *Wan Ling Record* states that out of a thousand or ten thousand candidates only three or perhaps five succeed in passing the Gate—the only known statistics on the subject, supplied by the most qualified authority during the peak of the Zen movement (i.e. between 0.3 per cent and 0.05 per cent, or 1 in 333 and one in 2,000). These statistics are supported by the evident difficulty experienced by the Fifth Patriarch in finding a successor other than the apparently unsuitable and illiterate Corean youth who did not reach maturity until fifteen years after the Patriarch's death. At the same time it would appear that from the times of Bodhidharma until Hui Neng the teaching of the One Mind remained essentially a "secret" doctrine, reserved for those few who could "take" it, for, otherwise, the story of the persecution of Hui Neng is incomprehensible.

There can be no doubt, therefore, that the term was applied to purely intellectual comprehension as well as to the pure spiritual realisation which the term implies to us in this context. More probably it was a generic term, as, in fact, it is in colloquial English, and had no technical limitation whatever.

We should bear this in mind, for we have been led astray, here as about "meditation," and considerable confusion and misunderstanding have resulted.

REALITY AND MANIFESTATION

91 ᵡ *The Essential Explanation - I*

Every appearance is a concept in Mind.
Every appearance is also a suchness in Reality.
Every appearance is a concept of a suchness
That can never be an object of perception.

PHYSICS AND METAPHYSICS

92 ᵡ *Do We Know How to Read?*

Why do we understand so little of what we read? I can suggest one reason. Most of us read more novels than anything else when we were young. Some of us still do. You know how we read novels. Some of us read them in a day, others in a week. Later in life a few of us re-read one or two of them. That is apt to remain our idea of "reading," our habit, our technique. And that is why our books are so wordy, why what can be said in ten pages is said in two hundred.

Do we read the Masters like that? From cover to cover, and then put them away? What? You re-read the Diamond Sutra again not so long ago? Did you? And Huang Po also? How well you must know them now! But may I point out to you that when you have read any of them at intervals for the thirtieth time, and not necessarily from cover to cover, you will have understood more of them each time—and the thirty-first time most of all.

A man can read through a book and not fully comprehend one idea that is expressed therein. Or he can, to all intents, find himself within the mind that was dictating the text to his fingers. How often are readers nearer the latter extreme than the former?

REALITY AND MANIFESTATION

93 ·— Is It a Concept?

Looking around one it is quite evident that the significance of Huang Po's repeated statement about the use of mind has not been grasped. We have pointed out that the reason "You cannot use mind to seek mind" (*Chün Chou Record,* 14) is that we *are* mind, and that therefore there is nothing to seek, "mind" being the term the T'ang Masters preferred while pointing out that no such thing really exists. To us "mind" is apt to be confusing, and "reality" is more in our idiom. "How can you use mind to perceive (or reach or grasp) mind?" he asks again in the *Wan Ling Record,* 37. How can an eye see itself? we have asked. And all the Masters have told us that there is nothing to grasp anyway. Huang Po usually adds, by way of explanation, "or the Buddha to seek the Buddha," "or the Dharma to seek the Dharma," "formlessness to grasp formlessness," "void to grasp Void," "the Way to grasp the Way"; he neglects nothing in his desire that we should understand. I have tried to show that I-subject is the Buddha, or the Buddha-nature, in Western idiom. There is nothing to seek or to reach or to grasp, neither our own actual face nor our "original face"—for we have both already, just as we have "enlightenment" but fail to notice it.

But there is another sense in Huang Po's statement about mind, one which needs emphasis. We cannot use our psyche either in order to seek, reach, attain or grasp "mind." We cannot use any concept in order to perceive mind. No object in consciousness can do that. One would need an adding-machine in order to tot up the number of times all the Masters have told us that the conceptualisation process stands in our way, and that until we can by-pass that we cannot hope to get anywhere—not in aeons as numerous as those over-used and hard-worn grains of sand in the Ganges.

Cannot we make up our minds to believe them? We don't really know what they mean? And anyhow we haven't a ghost of a notion of how to do it? "I think, therefore I exist," we echo Descartes. Yes, indeed. Yes, indeed, alas, alas! I think, therefore I think I am an ego! I think I am an ego, therefore I think! But the intellect is a machine, and often a serviceable one; the electronic variety can do better, but ours is adequate for our real needs. Has our intuition not made it clear that our intellectual machine can never reveal Mind? In between thoughts, *we can know ourselves as Mind.* By suppressing thoughts? Never on your life! Just leave them alone.

And as for manipulations of the psyche as means to the end . . . springes to catch wodecockes!

Let us ask ourselves each time, "Is it a concept?" If so—we have lost our way.

94 ·- Quiddity

Envy, hatred and malice, greed, anger and violence are just names we give to symptoms, as a result of analytical thought.

Each one has its counterpart, and part and counterpart constitute one whole. In psychology they are termed positive and negative feeling, in ethics good and evil. All are just names. All are just concepts. None exists in reality.

As long as we discriminate between good and evil we are still tied up in the net of conceptualism, which is duality. We can experience positivity rather than negativity, and vice versa according to circumstances, but, since they are one and the same notion, the difference lies in the manner of interpretation.

People who have never heard of metaphysics are apt to tell you that love and hate are the same thing, and can be transmuted. The fact has become apparent without knowledge of the principle. But they want the one only, the one without, or rather than, the other, and they do not see the absurdity of that: one part of a pair of opposites cannot exist without the other, nor one element of complementaries, for each only exists, even apparently, in function of the other.

The transmutation of hate into love effects nothing, for both are on the same plane. Hate merely becomes selfish possessive love, accompanied by jealousy and fear of loss of possession.

But if they are seen as one, if their identity is comprehended, they cease automatically to be interpreted as either—they re-become what they really are. Since we must give everything a name in order that it may appear to exist, let us call it pure feeling.

But pure feeling has its quota of names also; it is *karuna* and *caritas*—detached, impersonal, unpossessive love, which looks like compassion, benevolence, kindness, all of which are dualistic notions resulting from an intellectual analysis of positive feeling, none of which it is, since none of which really exists, for they are names for concepts.

Yes, you are right of course, *karuna-caritas* is a concept also, and it is part of a duality. Its counterpart is *prajna*, usually translated as transcendental wisdom, though "pure understanding" or just "insight" may be more helpful. But if we can see those two as one, if we can unite part and counterpart so that we recognise and know what that is—we have transcended duality.

No, don't try to give it a name. Suchness must be eternally nameless.

Note: Karuna represents the affective (emotional) aspect of this basic duality, of which the counterpart is the intellectual aspect termed *prajna*.

In our formula the components of each group are concepts that are objects in consciousness, experienced via I-dream-subject. *Prajna* and *karuna* are objects in consciousness experienced by I-subject whom I have also termed the Imperson.

95 ·— Reverence—A Causerie

Reverence is commonly regarded as a virtue. Probably it is. On the social plane of our daily lives it has evident advantages, although it may sometimes raise a smile. For actors, playing our parts in the comedy of apparent existence, it is surely an agreeable characteristic.

Metaphysically regarded, however, it is an unequivocal sign of identification with the notion of an ego. It betrays our state of bondage every time it is manifested. For only a supposed ego could experience such a sentiment, so that such sentiment is necessarily the manifestation of a supposed ego, that is, a manifestation resulting from the role of an assumed "personality."

That Zen takes every opportunity of jeering at reverence, as opposed to all the popular religions which encourage it, is evidence of Zen's superior penetration and doctrinal purity: it is uncompromising and makes no concessions.

The anecdotes of the burning of statues of the Buddha for firewood, of rinsing the mouth after mentioning a "sacred" name, of turning aside if you should happen to meet him and at all costs not stopping to salute him, are all devised to the end of eradicating the notion of reverence as something to be cherished. However, they make an unfortunate impression on Western ears, for they tend to appear as examples of sheer bad manners the object of which is not directly revealed in the story. That such an interpretation is gratuitous is evident in view of the respect given to, and exacted by, the Masters themselves, and in the respectful manner in which they quote the "Blessed One." For not only superficial reverence is attacked in these stories, but also reliance on an apparent "person."

One anecdote, however, is at the same time more revealing and more amusing—that in which a monk visiting an anchorite in a forest jumps nervously at the roar of a wild beast in the vicinity, and is told by the hermit, "I see it is still with you!" While the latter enters his cave in search of some refreshment, the visitor scratches the name of the Buddha on the rock on which his host has been sitting. Returning, and about to resume his seat, the hermit sees the "holy" name and remains standing; whereupon the visitor remarks sardonically, "I see it is still with you also!"

And did not the Bodhidharma himself reply to the question of the Emperor Wan Li, in the course of the famous interview, when asked to expound the ultimate meaning of the holy doctrine: "Emptiness, Majesty, and no holiness in it anywhere!"

PHYSICS AND METAPHYSICS
96 ·- Being

The Present is in fact the immutable state of being which we enjoy without apprehending it in the intervals between thoughts (i.e. mental activity of any kind). These intervals are outside time—which is a by-product of mental activity; are frequent, at every second moment, so to speak, in the time sequence; and, outside the time sequence, of infinite, or of zero, duration.

This is the permanent state of being in which we really are, and which is the immutable background of our phenomenal lives. To apprehend it is surely Awakening.

It follows that "we" normally can know no Present.

Homo Sapiens

Is it not strange that man, who thinks himself superior to his fellow-creatures, despite all evidence to the contrary, should place himself below their level by destroying them not for nourishment but for amusement?

Karuna-Caritas

This insight in which love and hate are seen as one, as what we are only able to see as positive, as a "chemically" pure kind of love, is not a result to be obtained by concentration or effort of any kind. It occurs automatically if the notion of an individual, of a feeler of love and of hate, is eliminated.

The self as lover or hater abolished, the emotion which is their reality is revealed in its pristine purity, as what it really is. And that is what appears to us as *karuna-caritas*.

143

The Present

The only self is the Present: the only Present is the self-Unself or I-Reality. The Eternal Present and the Unself are one.

97 ·~ *The Possibility of Reincarnation*

Since dualism cannot exist without thought; since Time is an effect of dualism; and since any reincarnation must inevitably be subject to Time, it follows that whatever could reincarnate must be capable of thought. This finds confirmation in the universal belief that those who have transcended the thinking process are thereby liberated and for ever free from the process of reincarnation. But thought requires a somatic apparatus by means of which to find expression, so that what is involved in reincarnation can only be the principle of thought, which expresses itself via one and then another somatic apparatus of genetic origin.

What do we understand by the principle of thought? It is evidently an element of what we term the psyche, an element that is not normally recognisable apart from other elements. It should be responsible for memory, since but for memory it is doubtful if Time could be experienced. I think we may be certain also that it should be responsible for desire, which we sometimes call "will," and this is supported by the frequent statement that desire is responsible for reincarnation.

Further we may assume that the principle of thought operates as what we now recognise as a force-field, of an electronic nature, and that its manifestation in the physical universe is by means of what we know as vibrations, probably of a high frequency.

Such a principle might be capable of carrying over reflections or echoes of past mundane experience, nostalgias, tendencies, prophetic knowledge of "future" mundane experience, eagerness for them or dread of them, and even physical reminiscences or anticipations that find expression via the somatic structure! But the most important baggage element in each successive transfer would seem to be what is called *karma*—the residue in a time-context of the resultants of all actions performed during a "life."

The principle of thought should be the controlling factor of the psyche, but an influence rather than an entity, in fact just what we have called it—a principle, and it cannot have in itself anything resembling what we recognise as a personality or individuality, since it is by definition a principle only. In the perspective of Reality it is merely a concept, an object in Consciousness, and it has no absolute existence.

Let us rest content for the present with the term Principle of Thought that is associated with a series of specific psychosomatic apparatuses, and the term for the transformation itself, if it exists, should not be "Reincarnation" but "Transmigration."

REALITY AND MANIFESTATION

98 ⸱⸱ *I Am, or the Ultimate Subject*

All objectivity, as such, is unreal—except in that, being integral in consciousness, it must be a derivative of reality therein.

It follows that all subjectivity, as such, is real—except when, being envisaged and so becoming a concept, it is thereby an object, and so—unreal, which is the process of identification, which produces the supposition of an ego.

❦

This, in other terms, is a restatement of the view that the ego-notion is the attribution of subjectivity to an object in consciousness. (*The Fact of the Matter,* Ch. 69)

In setting forth that view some difficulty was encountered in describing the withdrawal of subjectivity from the object: the intuition remained incomplete.

This restatement reveals the process as automatic, for when the subject is envisaged as such, and so becomes an object, the real subject, the observer, remains, untouched by the process, and can never be affected by any object or process of objectivisation (conceptualisation). I AM is eternally present, eternally real, the ultimate subject, subjectivity itself, and all that is.

As long as I know myself as I AM there can be no object in existence, no identification, and no idea of an ego.

Note 1: "No object in existence?" A hard saying? Perhaps, but *so it must be.*

Note 2: It may be objected that it is the transcendence of the duality subject-object that is real, and not one element in that duality. The answer is given in the Table entitled *Metaphysical Analysis of What We Are,* Ch. 81: the transcendence of the Dividual or I-dream-subject/object, i.e. their reality, is termed therein the Imperson or I-subject, and the transcendence of I-subject/all objects is termed therein the Unself or I-Reality. Subject, as such, always being real, only its pseudo or conceptual aspect can ever be transcended.

The terminology, then, is faulty? Yes, indeed; but can terminology do more than suggest? If we substitute "I-pseudo-subject" for "I-dream-subject," and "I-observing-subject" for "I-subject" will that be more helpful? Good, then let us do so.

Note 3: What *is* reality anyhow? That which is immutable.

Note 4: The transcendence of any duality is represented by the I-observer who alone constitutes the relation between the two independent objects in consciousness of which the duality is composed. This point is clearly brought out by John Levy in his *The Nature of Man According to The Vedanta,* though he must not be held responsible for my use of it.

99 ᴗ *Transcendence—What It Is*

The point just made may be explained as follows.

Since no two thoughts can occur simultaneously, the only relation between any two objects in consciousness must be represented by the observer of them.

Sensorial perceptions occur by means of a psycho-somatic apparatus to which the perception is attributed, by identification, as subject. But the supposed subject is itself an object, so that the two objects remain quite unrelated except via the observer, who alone observes them both.

The transcendence of duality, therefore, is represented simply, and exclusively, by the observing consciousness.

The Observer is, of course, just the consciousness in which objects appear.

PHYSICS AND METAPHYSICS

100 ᴗ *The Wrath of God*

People who are unused to abstract thought are apt to be unaffected by the apparent contradiction involved in belief in a God of Mercy who in effect can be observed to be merciless.

People who think occasionally of abstract matters are apt to be profoundly shocked by the cruelty of God towards His devoted creatures. In some this takes the form of indignation, in others of disbelief in the existence of such a deity.

To people who think habitually in the abstract it is obvious that, mercy and mercilessness constituting a dualism, God must necessarily be both merciful and merciless in our eyes—that is just God.

Furthermore they will ask themselves to *whom* God is either merciful or merciless? And they will perceive that such person or persons—and God appears merciful and merciless to large numbers as readily as to an individual—can only be the imaginary entity conceived as a result of identification of I-reality with a psyche-soma, i.e. the pseudo-I or ego-notion. That is to say, the effects of mercy and mercilessness are applied to an entity or entities that have no existence in reality. God is praised for being merciful, blamed for being merciless, to a mere concept, a dream-figure.

Still further they will observe that God is being supplied with attributes—for mercy and mercilessness are such—and how could God have attributes? The notion is surely primary?

But who is this God anyhow? Is He not the reality of the psyche-soma concerned? Is He not the reality of that which praises God for his mercy and blames Him for His mercilessness? When one looks within, instead of without, will he not find himself face-to-face with—himself?

Note: I am confusing the Creator-and-his-creatures with Godhead Itself, the former being the dual aspect of the latter? Yes, indeed. But I can quote authority—popes and pastors, prophets and people. No excuse? Sorry. Does it really matter? Are not both Subject?

101 ·- Transcendence or Neutralisation?

Writers seem to concur in urging us to transcend duality. Such concurrence is rare and impressive. But do not opposites rather cancel one another—leaving the thing itself, i.e. its suchness?

Transcendence implies the surpassing of two things, and the consequent attainment of a third thing. But there are no "things" in reality, of any kind whatever: there is only the thing-in-itself, its suchness, which is Reality, revealed when the illusory dualism of inexistent qualities is dissolved.

Have we understood this? Neither Love nor Hate can exist as such, since each is a function of the other. When it is perceived that they cancel one another out they disappear, and that which is left is pure affectivity, which is not another "thing" but the suchness of both, and a name for that which to us appears as one aspect of reality.

☙

Perhaps the importance of this observation lies in the fact that transcendence implies an effort, where no effort is called for or could effect anything, whereas the neutralisation of opposites and complementaries is automatic when perceived, and merely renders account of a state of affairs that eternally is. And that is the real understanding that matters.

102 ·- Duality or Dualism?

Although there appears to be little justification etymologically, there is a useful convention in French whereby the term *dualité* is reserved for that which is personal, whereas the term *dualisme* is reserved for that which is not, i.e. for qualities, attributes, and states of mind.

Thus subject-and-object represent a duality, whereas good-and-evil, love-and-hate, represent dualisms.

It may be helpful to follow this convention?

Personal

Why do I call myself a Buddhist? If it should be necessary to attach oneself to any denomination, and in daily life there may be circumstances which render that necessary, Buddhism is the only religion which is large enough, in spirit and in practice, to include all the others.

REALITY AND MANIFESTATION

103 ⸺ The Essential Explanation - II

Since the dawn of history well-intentioned people have devised systems whose aim was to save the world by means of love. Less ambitious people have never tired of seeking personal salvation by the same means. But how could anything be achieved by love?

Do not love and hate constitute one whole? Can they be separated? It would be like walking upstairs with one foot remaining on the ground. The same kindly optimists advise their fellows to conquer hate by love. But can treble counter base? You can thump one set of keys harder, that is all.

In order that what these well-intentioned people seek may be achieved it should be necessary to transcend both love and hate—since they are one. But that too surely is just a romantic notion, for who is there to transcend what, and by what means? The human will? Springes to catch wodecockes!

Love and hate cannot be experienced simultaneously, any more than any thoughts or emotions: how can two independent perceptions be transcended? But if we regard them one after the other, realising that they are one, we can see that they cancel one another and so cease to appear to exist as either the one or the other. What is left is neither, but just affectivity, pure affectivity, the essence of both. Love and hate are powerless, except in imagination since they are works of imagination: pure affectivity is unlimited in power—since it is the atmosphere of reality itself. That is what they mean who seek to save the world, or themselves, by means of love. But never could they do it by what they know as love, alone, which is as powerless as any dream-gesture. They may cite great teachers, but such teachers surely knew the truth and, alas, their words have passed through many mouths and have been deformed by many hands, disciples who only partially understood.

❧

Pure affectivity, however, is not reality itself, but only one element of a dual aspect thereof. The complementary element is pure cognition.

Knowledge and ignorance represent a duality that cancels out like love and hate, leaving an essence that we may term pure cognition, which is as powerful as pure affectivity, being also an aspect of reality. But, like that, it is not reality itself, but one element of a dual aspect thereof.

Just as reality cannot be experienced by the emotion of love, renamed for the occasion devotion, which is the flaw in all dualistic religions, so reality cannot be experienced by intellectual means, called knowledge in this context. This is, no doubt, the explanation of so many failures on the part of the only saintly or the only wise.

These two dual aspects of reality itself, which I have termed pure affectivity and pure cognition, *karuna* and *prajna*, must also be "transcended" in order to integrate reality. But even here two independent percepts cannot be experienced simultaneously, and so cannot in effect be "transcended," not even by the concepts that we are! They must be seen as complementaries, and they too must be seen as one whole.

That is surely the nameless reality that the Buddha knew.

❧

Discouraging? Whyever? Anyone who has read this book so far should be able to dispose of the twin notions of love-and-hate, knowledge-and-ignorance, in that twinkling of the mind that is called intuition. Having arrived thus at a realisation of pure-affectivity-and-pure-cognition, we have only to lay ourselves open to that awareness which ignores thought— for the final comprehension is not a concept but just the essence of consciousness.

We cannot seize it? Of course not: we are it.

104 ⸗ Reincarnation: Ultimate Observation

Speaking in a general manner it may be said that almost every point of view favours the idea of reincarnation—or transmigration as it is less inadequately termed—except one.

It is explicitly accepted by almost the whole of the Eastern and wiser half of the world, and none of the Masters has ever denied it: it is taken for granted by wise and simple, and the Sages frequently refer to it as a fact. But against it there is one apparently insuperable objection. The central or pivotal element in the doctrine of the Buddha, and the fundamental belief of everyone who has ever fully understood that doctrine, results from the realisation that no entity has ever existed, exists, or ever could exist, and that therefore there is nothing, could not be anything, that could incarnate, reincarnate, or transmigrate in any circumstances whatsoever!

We all understand this, I hope. Anyone who has read this book must be familiar with the details of this apparently formidable contradiction. But let us consider this matter once more, and in the simplest possible manner.

What can we imagine "reincarnating" anyhow? Anything might reincarnate if there is anything to reincarnate, but unless it were potentially identifiable as having incarnated already it could never be known as having done so, and the very idea would be meaningless. Nothing, however, can fulfill this essential condition but that which has the notion of self. In other words—if anything can "reincarnate," that thing must be, or must be accompanied by, the I-notion.

But—and who knows it better than we do by now?—what is the I-notion? It is a concept. And a concept is not an entity. Do we know what becomes of a concept? When an I-concept finds the body decaying that it supposed was itself, what does it do, what becomes of it?

I do not, of course, know; nor, I presume, do you; but being subject to Time, why should it not attach itself to another nascent body, if it can find one? And might it not be attracted to one with inherent, or genetical, similarities to the one that has left it high-and-dry by dissolution? Whatever it be in metaphysics—a minute electronic force-field in flux, a fluctuating vibrational complex, might it not be associated with residual experience which it could bring over and deposit in the psyche-soma in which it has found a new

153

home? If that reads like a description of an entity, the fault is mine: it is not an entity in the sense of the Buddha, any more than is a cloud or a smell or an electric storm.

What may have occurred is like any other occurrence in the "waking" dream of manifestation. The concept-complex had a discrete existence in illusory time, as an object of a dream-subject, and, after an instantaneous experience of timelessness on the dissolution of its past, associated body-object, it became attached to another nascent body-object and re-entered the sequential or time-illusion.

Note A: Let us remember that all our lives are timeless as well as in time. Time is only an interpretation, in apparent sequence, of the intemporal.

Note B: The alternative notion that each nascent body-object develops its own I-notion literally *ab ovo* is quite gratuitous, and is contradicted by many recorded actions of the very young.

Note C: We know from all the Masters that liberation from "birth-and-death," that is, from rebirth, is consequent on liberation from the ego or I-notion, *which implies that the I-notion is itself the essential factor in that process.*

Note D: Let us be careful not to confuse the I-notion, an object in consciousness, with any degree of I-subject, which is real in whatever degree of apparent limitation. The I-notion is just a notion of "selfness," as an object it can do nothing but be an apparent I—as a jug can only be an apparent jug.

Its transference, or transmigration, from soma to soma, or body-object to body-object, would be just that and nothing more. Transmigration does not mean that you or I transmigrate in reality—which would be impossible nonsense—but just that the absurd notion with which we identify ourselves does that! There could only be "reincarnation" of that—but never of anything that is real.

154

Note E: The only importance of this process would seem to be that as long as the identification goes on in time we *appear* to go on in time, and on and on and on; the *fantoche* lives and re-lives "for ever," that is, until it rids itself of the notion that *it* is I. At that moment only the appearance remains—for then we are real and know it, that is, we know our timeless reality and the *fantoche* for what it is. Perhaps it may be found that it is only in explanation of this, or in a context that implies it, that the Masters refer to "reincarnation" or "transmigration"?

So understood—have we perhaps begun to understand this apparent contradiction despite which "the dream goes on"?

105 ⸱⁓ *The Essential Explanation - III: The Big Black Cloud*

TWO: You say there is an imbalance between my Affectivity and my Cognition; what does that mean exactly?

ONE: Imbalance between your resolution of two sets of dualisms: between Knowledge-Ignorance and Love-Hate.

TWO: You mean I have some Pure Cognition, less Pure Affectivity?

ONE: You may well have: it is not uncommon over here.

TWO: So what?

ONE: All this minor affectivity: liking and disliking; all this major affectivity: loving and hating. Stop discriminating, *see* them as one whole, and then you'll *feel* them as Pure Affectivity.

TWO: I'll try. Anything else?

ONE: You can surrender.

TWO: How do? Surrender what, by what, to whom?

ONE: The notion of your precious pseudo-self. Some

people do it to God. But it is only the surrendering itself that is relatively real. The French *se rendre* seems better.

TWO: How can I surrender myself? My precious pseudo-self notion has no suicidal tendencies that I have noticed.

ONE: Your precious pseudo-self notion is never the doer— you know that, there is no do-er, no deed, only a do-ing. How many times? . . .

TWO: Not so many as some other things, but I remember it nevertheless. Who tells us that?

ONE: All of them by implication, a few explicitly.

TWO: Puzzling all the same: no one to do it, no one to receive it.

ONE: I have said that your idea of a pseudo-self cannot *do* anything. Your reality does not act except by non-action. But, if you want to, you can surrender to Jumbo, to me, to God, or to this glass of wine: that is purely incidental. Do it: the doing is all that matters.

TWO: But something must do it, damn it all!

ONE: What could there be to do it? The illusion of a do-er is the big black cloud. When you have seen that doer and deed only exist as a doing, you will have arrived at a vital understanding.

TWO: In a flash of intuition?

ONE: There is no other way. Stop thinking; stop, I tell you! [he drops the glass with a crash].

TWO: I see it, I see it: there is only DOING! What else could there be? Ha-ha-ha! Is it not obvious?

ONE: As obvious as the moon when the big black cloud has passed.

106 ·~ Perception and Reality

There is nothing perceptible about enlightenment, or about the reality, the suchness, of anything. "Let me repeat," says Huang Po, "that the perceived cannot perceive." That means that in so far as we are perceived, or perceptible, that aspect of what we regard as us cannot perceive either.

Then what does perceive? Perception itself, yourself as perception, for your reality is that and not a "person." "Your real nature and your perception of it are one," says Huang Po, again. You cannot use it in order to see beyond it, for you are it. Perception itself cannot perceive itself as "enlightened."

So in our ephemeral aspect we can neither perceive enlightenment itself nor our own permanent state of enlightenment. Anyone who thinks he perceives himself as such can only be a victim of his ego-notion.

That is another way of understanding that what we imagine as "enlightenment" does not exist as such, that is as something we-as-we-think-we-are can attain or become. Rather the reality of "enlightenment" is just ourselves as we are in reality.

Direct Cognition

It can never be by means of our intellectual apparatus, which we think of as "our minds," that we can apprehend non-duality. Direct cognition, intuition if you prefer the term, or *bodhi*, cuts out that mechanism. The intellectual apparatus may indeed itself be the responsible agent of the phenomenon of dualism.

Nor can direct cognition be invoked, as far as we know. Only can we invoke a state of Awareness in which it can function, or via which we can become conscious of it.

107 ·— One Half of a Pair—A Causerie

"Beware of clinging to one half of a pair (of opposites)." (Huang Po, *Wan Ling Record*, 54)

Is not this the hidden barrier on the path of Western pilgrims?

In Zen particularly, comprehension appears to be all-important. It is stressed to the apparent exclusion of devotion. Yet it is in fact one half of a pair. But one half of a pair is a dualism, and reality cannot be integrated dualistically.

Even in Vedanta Advaita, as represented by the Maharshi, nearly all his answers to questions urged comprehension by some form of the query "Who am I?" Only perhaps to those intellectually unfitted to follow that quest did he urge surrender, which represents the other "half of the pair."

Yet when one reads his biographies, and accounts of him, the non-intellectual aspect of the state in which he lived is very evident. We interpret it as "kindness"—for that is the guise in which it appears to us. He was never what we call "sentimental," for that implies the notion of a pseudo-ego, which he had no longer, but his immense kindness or compassion—and its immensity is often stressed—was his biographers' interpretation of pure affectivity, the counter-aspect of pure understanding, for we can only perceive the awakened state dualistically.

In Zen there is little sign of affectivity, yet there also the immense "kindness" of the Masters is obvious. Indeed even their rough methods, including the "thirty blows," are examples of that kindness, and are recognised as such in the texts. There seems to have been no care or effort they spared themselves in order to bring their disciples to enlightenment, that is, in order to wake them up, save discourse or argument—which they knew to be commonly a hindrance and hardly in any circumstances a help.

How are we to understand this? Just as the intellection of discourse and argument is "one of a pair," so is any kind of human sentiment. All these dualisms must be resolved. But we cannot have two thoughts at the same time, so how can we "transcend" any pair of opposites or complementaries? We inevitably perceive one, and then the other, so that they remain separate and independent objects in consciousness. The Zen Masters would have us "in a flash of thought" see both as one, but what is translated as a "flash of thought" is surely the flash of a short-circuit which cuts out thought. It is pure intuition, direct cognition, which cannot occur when thought itself is occurring.

Where there is no discrimination there is no attachment, and then neither love nor hate can occur, nor can knowledge *or* ignorance occur, and even pure affectivity *and* pure cognition are one and the same thing, so that it is only as seen by us in the guise of thoughts that they appear dualistically, in a double aspect as the one, and then as the other, two independent incompatible percepts.

It seems to follow that we can never have the unitary cognition by concentrating on either element of the pair, but only by ridding ourselves of both. But pure affectivity and pure cognition are beyond our reach as long as we are subject to the illusion of individuality—that ultimate barrier, the difficulty, well nigh insuperable, in the East as in the West, to all but an infinitesimal minority, of realising that they themselves do not exist as individuals.

First we need to rid ourselves of love-and-hate, and of knowledge-and-ignorance, which, resolved, leave us with pure affectivity and pure cognition, the dual aspects of just being (if we must give it a word symbol). Since we cannot merge notions that occur independently and in sequence in consciousness, since we cannot fuse two elements that cannot come into contact—then it can only remain for us to dissolve them one after the other, and that by comparing them and perceiving their mutual exclusiveness in a context of total interdependence. How can either exist by itself, as "one of a pair"? It cannot: therefore it does not exist. It is dissolved! Both are dissolved! And what is left, what takes their place? Intuition, direct cognition, reveals to us their *reality!* No longer is there love-and-hate, but just pure affectivity; no longer is there knowledge-and-ignorance, but just pure cognition; the reality of which is their thusness (see *Notes A* and *C).*

But what is the answer to the apparent problem, that of a Zen technique which seems to us to rely exclusively on understanding and not at all on emotion? We have understood above that in the awakened state of the Masters, which is also potentially our own, there is no dualistic difference between the cognitive and affective aspects between which we habitually discriminate, yet as long as we so discriminate we remain subject to dualism and asleep. Can we understand by *prajna* alone, ignoring *karuna?*

Can we believe that it could be so? Pure affectivity must be present in consciousness in order that pure cognition may be present, and if pure cognition and pure affectivity are to be resolved in what we have signalised as the thusness of being—both must be present, for in no dualism can one element be absent, any more than can an object from the shadow it casts. Perhaps this is the answer? Pure affectivity is there all the time? Of course it should be; were it not there pure cognition could not be there either. But is pure cognition there? Perhaps not. Is that not the barrier? And why is it not? Because pure affectivity is not there!

Is it not up to us to see that both are there? Perhaps the

Chinese monk in the ninth century did not need this reminder. Anyhow, how much do we know of what he did or was told? Quite certainly we have not a complete picture. And we are not he, in our dualistic aspect at least.

Perhaps in order to realise Zen we need this adjustment that to the Chinese would have been superfluous?

Note A: "Knowledge destroys knowledge—this knowledge invalidates that knowledge—and then no knowledge remains for you to grasp." (Huang Po, *Wan Ling Record,* 41) "Transcendental knowledge invalidates relative knowledge" (translator's note).

Note B: How do we correct imbalance between cognition and affectivity? Vedanta teaches it. You are too resolute a Buddhist? But is that frame of mind truly buddhistic? Never mind: just surrender (*se rendre*) absolutely.

Note C: The dualism "Knowledge-Ignorance" is liable to misunderstanding. In *The Essential Explanation - II,* Ch. 103, I used the terms "Knowledge and Ignorance." What is meant, both there and here, is "Knowledge" dualistically expressed, that is capable of verbal formulation, but based on an understanding of the relation of Reality (noumenon) and phenomena, whereas "Ignorance" and "Intellection" refer to the results of reasoning based on the supposition that the phenomenal world is real.

The dualism concerned is definitely not between transcendental knowledge which cannot be expressed in dualistic language, and all kinds of phenomenal knowledge which can. Transcendental Knowledge is "Pure Cognition" in this vocabulary, which represents the resolution of the dualism "Knowledge and Ignorance."

Note D: As pointed out in *Transcendence,* Ch. 99, all dualisms are related via the Observing consciousness, and find their resolution therein. In that Observing consciousness they only exist in a state of resolution. But in order to realise the Observer the elimination of the I-notion is necessary. This can be regarded as an alternative approach.

WORK AND PLAY

108 ·- Democracy - II

"Democracy" is a contradiction in terms—which perhaps accounts for its inefficacy, its indignity, and its injustice. If people were able to govern themselves they would not need governing at all. If they do not know how to govern themselves how can they govern one another?

In fact that is never attempted—not even on the small scale of clubs, in which by definition a degree of homogeneity exists. "Democracy" is misinterpreted to mean rule by parties, by conflicting ideologies, in which theories and principles replace men. The people vote for men, but the men they vote for are merely representatives and servants of dogmas. We know, however, that in an ephemeral, constantly changing world dogmas are *ipso facto* false, and that only immediate response, spontaneous reaction to circumstances, can ever succeed. The one is dead, the other alive.

If power is necessary, power must be delegated; if power is delegated it should be exercised by a living man and not by the representative of a dead dogma.

Ends and Means

The theory that ends justify means is senseless in view of the fact that they are two aspects of one thing. When means are violent and fraudulent the doctrine and its application must necessarily be so also. When means are rational and moderate that which they seek to establish is so too. When a

162

doctrine is transmitted subtly "from mind to mind by mind"—that doctrine is inevitably the doctrine of Mind.

109 ·— Dusting the Parrot

TWO: I am in a hat.

ONE: Take it off.

TWO: Devotion is dualist. One is devoted to a deity.

ONE: Love and hate are dualist. One loves and hates something.

TWO: But the way of Knowledge is not?

ONE: Of course it is: its counterpart is Ignorance.

TWO: So both "ways" are dualist?

ONE: Of course.

TWO: I have been led astray.

ONE: If you will read books. . . .

TWO: So Buddhism is dualist like Christianity and Islam? Even Zen is dualist?

ONE: In so far as they enunciate a doctrine they must be.

TWO: Phew!

ONE: It is the doctrine that is dualist, not the revelation.

TWO: But there is no such thing as love or hate?

ONE: Of course not.

TWO: Nor knowledge or ignorance?

ONE: Evidently.

TWO: Just as there is no doer or that which is done?

ONE: That is so.

TWO: But you speak of them.

ONE: I am not a sage, no more than you are.

TWO: I can't accept that, a little more at least, indeed a great deal more!

ONE: Not any more at all. Neither of us is a sage, and until we are, we are neither more nor less. But the practical reason is that unless we use current language we must keep silence, as some sages do.

TWO: But between ourselves cannot we do better?

ONE: We can try—provided we understand one another.

TWO: There is no lover and loved, but just loving? No knower and known, but just knowing? No doer and done, that is, deed, but just doing?

ONE: It would be nearer the truth to say that in each case, for all are one, the actor and the action are represented by the acting, being quite inexistent otherwise.

TWO: Then what are these things—love and hate, etc.?

ONE: Just names we give to our misinterpretations of reality.

TWO: But in their factual aspect?

ONE: Gestures, let us say. Like threatening the wind with clenched fists.

TWO: Then loving, knowing, doing are still not real?

ONE: As long as they are part of a pair of opposites they cannot be.

TWO: May I hit you very hard? Will you forgive me?

ONE: As long as the blow is not accompanied by loving or hating there will be nothing to forgive.

TWO: Subject and object, on which your whole system of metaphysics is built, seem to be in the same case as lover and loved, knower and known, doer and deed.

ONE: Subject and object are perfectly interchangeable with any of those except that they have a wider connotation and can be understood to include them all.

TWO: Instead of I-dream-subject and I-subject, I can speak of I-dream-lover, knower, doer, and, instead of I-subject, I-lover, knower, doer?

ONE: By all means. Devotionally-minded people may

prefer the first, rationalists the second, and men of action the third.

TWO: It is the "I" that matters, that is the constant factor from Reality to dream?

ONE: The "I" alone is real throughout, and remains entire throughout.

TWO: But just as doer and deed only exist as doing, as lover and loved only exist as loving, knowledge and known only exist as knowing—in what do subject and object only exist?

ONE: In existing itself.

TWO: And does existing exist?

ONE: As such—no. Not unless it IS.

TWO: IS being the resolution of that duality?

ONE: Of every duality.

TWO: But are not being and non-being a duality like any other?

ONE: Reality and non-Reality are also, like Tao and non-Tao. That is because dualistic language cannot be itself non-dual.

TWO: So we have to make some symbol of what we wish to convey by non-duality?

ONE: Non-duality is also "one half of a pair." What we mean cannot be expressed in word-symbols at all or by any means. We must keep silent, call it "X," or deliberately decide that a word such as Tao, Being, Absolute, One Mind, Principle of Consciousness, Reality, Non-duality, shall stand for what cannot be expressed by any word or combination of words.

TWO: And of these the verb to BE is the best?

ONE: There is no best. But there is no better!

TWO: We have seen that the state of Being, of Awakenedness, of Enlightenment, appears to us, who are in duality, as Pure Cognition and Pure Affectivity, and that Pure Cognition is the resolution of our dualism Knowledge and Ignorance, while Pure Affectivity is the resolution of what we feel as Love and Hate. Is not that so?

ONE: I agree.

TWO: We have also seen that Knowledge and Intellection only exist as Knowing and Thinking, and not at all as Knower and Known, Thinker and Thought; also that Love and Hate only exist as Loving and Hating, and not at all as Lover and Loved, Hater and Hated?

ONE: That is so, and it is important.

TWO: In what do Pure Cognition and Pure Affectivity really exist? They too cannot, I presume, be things-in-themselves?

ONE: There are no things-in-themselves.

TWO: Then what are they?

ONE: Pure Know*ing* and Pure Feel*ing*.

TWO: "Pure" meaning what we should describe as "chemically" pure, unmixed with anything whatsoever.

ONE: Yes, or, if you prefer, the Essence of Knowing and the Essence of Feeling. Better still, Essential Knowing and Essential Feeling. But you are driving language pretty hard; the poor old nag will scarcely stand up to such treatment: her hocks are none too sound.

TWO: But what alternative have I?

ONE: A simple one, the better: just understand.

REALITY AND MANIFESTATION

110 ·– Good-bye, Old Man

When one finally decides to abandon the notion of an "ego," to assist at the "death" of the "old man" and the birth of the "new," ought one not to say good-bye? After all, figment or not, one has lived with him all the days of one's conscious life, and in full conviction of his reality. More than that, one has identified oneself with him and firmly believed that one was he. Probably for most of the years, if anyone had thrown doubt on his existence one would have mentally consigned that person to a lunatic asylum.

The Japanese are said to have a graceful habit of interring an old pair of shoes that has served them well, and even a toothbrush, with a little burial service and a grateful farewell. How much better it would be if we had this charming habit; how much better *we should be* if we had it—instead of the stupid and arrogant way we have of throwing faithful old things away as though we were everything and they were nothing! Everything, no doubt, we are, but then so are they, and are they not as much or as little as we, and how much less vile!

In casting off our notion of an "ego" should we not give it a decent burial, if not a fond farewell? After all, however great a burden it has been, to whatever extent it has made our life hell, it has not been our enemy so much as our fate or our fault. Rather is it not like a prodigal son—who must be forgiven for whatever horrors and abominations he may have committed—just because he *is* our son?

So let us bid him farewell without ill-will. He has accompanied us throughout life, through thick and thin, loyally perhaps even though he may have been responsible for much of the thick and all of the thin. Let us give him a decent funeral!

But wait a minute! Don't let us forget how sly he is, how deceitful, how often he has duped us and played us up! If we make too much of a fuss of him, may he not show signs of life and return to destroy all our good work by resuscitating? That would be in his manner.

All things considered, let's not be sentimental, not even like the Japanese, graceful as their attitude may be towards that which they discard. Let us just be friendly and polite—and quite without ill-feeling for the past.

Let's just give him a wave of the hand, and say, "Good-bye, Old Man."

111 ·- Vale

As long as we try to approach Reality from the wrong direction—via our "selves"—how can we hope to reach it? Who is there to do that anyhow, except that which is phenomenal? Can phenomena reach noumenon? And what could there, then, be attained?

Only by recognising our impersonality can we know our reality, and apprehend our integration therein, then, so integrated, the phenomenal aspect of us will henceforth partake of its noumenon.

—W. W. W.

Colophon

Thereupon is attained the goal of the seeking,
and also the end of the search itself.
Then nothing more is there to be sought;
nor is there need to seek anything.

—PADMA SAMBHAVA

Why Lazarus Laughed

Since the beginning of recorded history, that is, since the composition of the Vedas and the building of the pyramids, man has striven incessantly to understand what he is. He is still striving, and always some of his finest intellects have been devoted to the search for an explanation. But never has he succeeded in finding the *kind of answer he sought,* and never can he succeed as long as his basic assumption is his own reality, that is, the reality of that which he assumes himself to be.

Yet the truth has been staring him in the face throughout this long period, for it is explicit in the *Upanishads* as in the Diamond Sutra; it is at least implicit in the *Baghavad Gita* and in the words attributed to Jesus; and it has been expressed as clearly as words can express it by the awakened sages of Vedanta, of Zen, and of Tantra. But in general man has found it too hard: he has not been able to face up to it, and he has turned away; resistance has been too strong, and the truth has appeared too difficult of credence, too lacking in verisimilitude because too little in accordance with appearances, and, let us admit, too humiliating to his conditioned pride.

But there have always been men who have understood,

though we may not have heard of them all or known their names; some we know, indeed many, such as the Maharshi, but there may be others whom we shall never recognise, for their outstanding characteristic should be the absence of any characteristic that is outstanding, and they are not necessarily called upon to teach.

Man seeks, and has always sought, to explain everything, from the universe to his own boots, by attributing it to an entity, and so lives in a world entirely peopled by entities. He is conditioned to interpreting everything his senses record in terms of supposed entities which therefore fill his horizon, so that they may be said to constitute his whole manner of thinking. And this man is asked to realise that all these entities are of his own invention, for no such thing as an entity has ever existed, or ever could exist, in any conceivable circumstances, anywhere in the cosmos! And foremost among these non-existent entities is that one which he supposes to be—*himself.*

Could anyone expect man to believe this? I hardly think so. Yet those who have taken the trouble, who have overcome the resistances, whose feeling for the truth has been stronger than either pride or prejudice, have come to see that not only may it be so but how and why it could not possibly be otherwise. Adaptation may not be immediate, for the resulting revaluation of values is ubiquitous and must be total, but, once the truth has been perceived as such, no further doubt is possible, and everything is seen as fundamentally simple.

Man, trying to understand what he is while assuming that he is something that he is not, is perhaps a subject for caricature, but let us not forget that we ourselves are that man! So when we realise the truth, when the understanding, crowding in upon us, bursts into flame and illumines our vision, what is our reaction? What could it be but an immense roar of laughter? If it is not that, if it is any other kind of reaction to knowledge—beware of it!

And when the laughter has died down—we can start starting to put our universe in order.

2

What I Am . . .

As ultimate subject I am all objects.

As relative subject I am the observer of a named object in consciousness.

As subject limited by the concepts of space and time I become identified with a named object which then appears to be an independent entity.

How I Realise What I Am

(1) When, as limited subject, I realise that the named object in consciousness is such only, identification ceases, and I am no longer limited. The conceptual bondage is over, and I know myself as relative subject and as observer of the associated named object.

(2) When, as relative subject, I realise that I and my associated object are one, I know myself as ultimate subject.

(3) Henceforward in so far as I manifest in the world of appearances as subject and named object, discontinuously but limited by space and time, I do so without identification with a supposed entity, and I no longer experience the bondage otherwise inherent in waking life. Free from inhibition and from suffering I live in obedience to cosmic law. However, in so far as I know myself as ultimate subject and all objects as concepts in pure consciousness which I am, I must be

omnipotent with regard to them.

Neither as ultimate subject nor in any degree of apparent limitation am I ever an entity, nor can any object be such, for nothing of the kind exists in the cosmos.

Note: Under identification, thinking as supposed object-entities, we conceive paragraphs 1 and 2 above in the reverse manner. We suppose that I, the object, the "me," succeed in identifying myself with the Observer (inevitably thereby another object-entity), and thus expect to be freed from inhibition. But that approach is an *impasse* and cannot lead anywhere, for the object is still seen as an entity endowed with subjectivity.

Until I realise that I am subject, and that the named, baptised, object is merely object and is devoid of subjectivity, I cannot escape from inhibition—for inhibition is the expression of that error.

3

I Am Not-I …

As unself I am pure consciousness—and nothing else whatever. There is nothing else I could be.

The sensorially perceived universe is entirely conceptual, composed of sensual images in consciousness, apparently real, as every category of dream appears real.

All degrees and categories of mental imagery, that is, all possible sensory experience, may be likened to localised ripples on the surface of an unlimited ocean which is consciousness.

The notion of entities, self-conscious or otherwise, and identification with them, forms part of this conceptual process, whose apparent disturbance of the surface of an otherwise immutable consciousness is an effect of the serial character of the time-illusion.

The conceptual universe is totally unreal regarded as a thing-in-itself, or as a complex of things-in-themselves, but it inevitably partakes of the reality in which it occurs—as every ripple is composed of water—which is the reality of pure consciousness itself, outside which there is nothing. That is to say that what is sensorially perceived and interpreted is not real at all as such, but that the perceiving itself is a mode of consciousness.

Only that which is real can be I and subject: all that which is unreal is not I and object, though the synthesis of subject and object is still I because I am not, and none such exists, but as pure consciousness ultimately I am necessarily everything.

You? You, of course, are I. And the alligator, and the ant. As entities we are nothing: as reality we are everything.

Have you understood?

Ischl. July 1959

4

Questions that Are Not

Why do all the ways and disciplines appear to be so complicated? Why do we encounter abstruse verbiage, and unending analysis, the splitting of hairs into innumerable fragments, names, qualities, divisions—in short continual discrimination? The truth itself, as the Sages have told us, is quite simple, and, for those who look in the right direction, perfectly obvious.

Is the reason for this not just that all this confusion is due to an heroic attempt to answer questions that are not such?

To questions that are based on false premises there can

never be an answer that is valid. How many of these questions, of which all this complicated verbiage is an attempted answer, are not primary, "simplistes," lacking in a dimension? Are they not based on false premises, like Dr. Hubert Benoit's example—"Why does the Eiffel Tower go for a walk in the Champ de Mars every morning at 9 o'clock?"

Another example is what is called "reincarnation," of which no acceptable explanation has ever been, or ever will be, offered as long as the answer is based on the supposition that there has ever been an in-carnation, and that a named entity can be reborn again and again as another named entity in a variety of genetically controlled carcases. Such a question is an "Eiffel Tower" based on a series of false assumptions.

In order to frame questions that are real it is desirable to begin by noting and excluding those whose premises are false, those which are primary and lacking in a dimension; then most of the remainder will need no answer, for they will be seen to carry their own in their pockets, and the residue will partake of the simplicity of the truth as perceived by the Masters.

The difficulty is to transcend the primary way of thinking and to acquire the ability to visualise apparent problems by means of a further direction of measurement and so of perception. But until we realise the necessity of that we are not likely to find the way.

Conversely, the reason why we read the explanations of the awakened Sages, often again and again, without apprehending the depth of their meaning, and so ignoring what they tell us as though we had not read it, is that same lack of the indispensable further dimension of vision whereby the truth of words immediately becomes obvious. Ultimately we develop it by the cultivation of intuition—and then we understand.

Meanwhile let us examine the questions we are asking, and perceive their inadequacy and the inadequacy of the complicated answers we and others seek to give them. How shall we know their inadequacy? By the complexity, and so the inadequacy, of the answers they are receiving!

5

The Hansom-Cab

Is it possible for a Buddhist to believe in the existence of a self in view of the categorical instructions of the Buddha himself not to cherish any such notion?

Yet Western Buddhists, at least, often speak and act as though they cherished that notion and regarded a self as factual.

But it is only possible to perceive its psychological existence, i.e. that it exists as a notion in the psyche. The attribution to it of any further degree of reality appears quite incredible.

Does it not follow that to cherish the notion would be gratuitous and even absurd?

And any endeavour to develop the personality via that notion must appear like attempting to perfect the hansom-cab.

The Unwanted Host

Some pilgrims find it so difficult to believe the Buddha and the Masters when they state and imply again and again that there can be no self, their resistance reasserts itself with such persistence and determination, that perhaps one should not neglect an opportunity of citing the greatest living authority on Buddhism, Dr. D. T. Suzuki:

"The correct statement is that in Zen there is no subject that experiences, nor is there any object that is experienced." (*Living By Zen*, p. 33)

It is only divided mind that supposes a self: to whole mind such a notion is meaningless. Is that not enough?

Straight from the Horse's Mouth

"The ego-self does not exist at all." (Maharshi, *Talks*, p. 454)

6

Time and Eternity

Eternity is the potentiality of all that is manifested in time.

Time is the analytical development of the potentiality which is eternity.

Living in the seriality of time we are also "living" eternity.

In precisely the same way, living in duality of mind we are at the same time living in the observing consciousness which is ultimately non-dual. The former is spurious: the latter real.

The conception of eternity as unending time is one of the popular notions that are primary and "simplistes," and that can never lead anywhere because they are based on false premises.

Who Is Sane?

How could man in dualism, with a split mind possibly be sane? "Normal" man, as has long ago been declared, is only man in the awakened state, who is presumed to have access to non-duality. "Abnormal" man, that is, man as we know him around us, can have no justifiable pretensions to sanity, and shows no evidence of having any.

Any sanity man may demonstrate surely comes direct from undivided mind.

Mind and Matter - I

The body seems to be a necessary element whereby mind can have experience.

If mind abandons matter—matter dissolves into its constituent elements.

Apart from matter there is no (dualistic) mind, but only non-dual mind of which both matter and dualistic mind are complementary manifestations. What we call "mind" and what we call "matter" are two aspects of one object in consciousness.

Mind

The impersonal observing consciousness, which we are, is ubiquitous, immanent, and transcendent. In no element of our composition is it absent. Our every experience is it.

7

Phenomenal Reality or the Reality of Phenomena

As a concept the reality of unicity (the One) is as false as the concept of the reality of duality (the pair).

The dual is always potentially unicity, and unicity is always potentially dual. They are not different.

Duality is not false as such—only as one element imagined

apart from its complement is it that. Duality as a whole, though dual, is potentially real.

Unicity is not false as such—only imagined as indivisible is it that. Unicity as infinitely multiple, though one, is real.

This may be implicit in Zen, for Professor Suzuki says, "Zen's position is always advaitistic, which means neither two nor one, but two in one and one in two." (*Living By Zen*, p. 109)

Faith

Faith is becoming a bamboo.

I Done It

The "I" is a separate thought, and it cannot be present at the moment of any action. The action is claimed by the I-notion as a subsequent thought: just as it might be claimed by a bystander.

Whatever action takes place is not performed by an "I." It is not performed by any entity. It is just an acting.

This is something that can be established by observation, that is, by experiment. Since we have been brought up to regard that as proof, let us note it again and again until we no longer imagine ourselves as doers.

This also applies to sensation, which is another mode of thought.

8

That We Are

The Buddha-mind is whole mind. It is not split. It is that

which we are. It is that aspect of the Absolute which is accessible to cognition. But it can only be apprehended subjectively, never as an object.

To apprehend subjectively means to know that we are it. This is not within the power of the reasoning intellect since there is no "it"—for "it" denotes an object. That apparatus must be left aside. In a state of pure awareness we may know by direct cognition that the Buddha-mind is us.

This whole mind or impersonal consciousness does not disown anything that we recognise as ourselves except the notion itself of "selves." It does not even "disown" that notion, rather does it not know it, for as long as that notion is with us we cannot know the Buddha-mind, that is, ourselves, and the Buddha-mind cannot know us as we think we are.

We can speak of it as an object, but that of which we so speak is not it. It is subject-object, but that we are unable to conceive. Therefore we cannot conceive it at all. We can only know it, and the only manner in which we can know it is as ourselves without any trace of "our" or any notion of "selves."

When we come to know the Buddha-mind, which is whole, we do not therefore cease to speak and act dualistically, for we cannot communicate with our fellows in any other manner. But it is the whole mind split that we use as such, and no longer just one half of a pair of complementaries without reference to the other. That is described as non-discrimination, nonattachment, and it is a result, not, as we often suppose, a method.

What is this state? We do not know it as anything but our natural state, or that it needs a name. In order that we may know that we are THAT WE ARE do we need to fulfill conditions and justify whatever a name may define? If reality is that which cannot be doubted, the knowledge that Buddha-mind is us is just that, and nothing can deprive us of knowledge of that which we are. There are half-a-dozen, and more, of such names, and they all necessarily describe personal experiences. But to know ourselves as *imperson* is not a personal experience.

Names follow us like shadows from various sources of light. Buddha-mind, Original-mind, the Unborn, the Inborn, Primary Nature, Heavenly Reason are just a few that are of Zen origin only. If they help us to recognise ourselves they fulfill their only function. As a description "impersonal consciousness" is clear also, since "it" is essentially consciousness and essentially impersonal; but "it" is also obviously our original mind, unborn, inborn, and the very nature of nature, as it is the mind of all the enlightened Sages.

9

What "It" Is

Where is the Impersonal Consciousness? No, it is not up there! Nor is it in my head, nor even in my heart or solar-plexus.

Regarded spatially and personally it is distributed in every cell of my anatomy.

Regarded psychically it might appear as a radionic aura.

Regarded impersonally it is immanent throughout space.

Regarded non-spatially it is infinity.

Regarded intemporally it is the eternal present.

Regarded temporally it is that which sees, hears, feels, tastes and smells. But "it" is never that which interprets perceptions.

My psyche-soma is the means whereby "it" manifests, and its manifestation is the justification of my psychesoma.

I am it, and it is I.

10

Whole-Mind

"That" of which we have been speaking as the Buddha-mind, with reference to several of its other names in Zen Buddhism, is whole mind, as opposed to half mind, mind split by the intellect into two halves, only one of which pair we are able to use at any one time, that is, as any one thought. In this dichotomy the seriality of time is a basic factor.

Another name for "it," familiar to Christians, is the name given it by Jesus in his allegorical manner of speech, the charming image of the "Father." In my analysis I have called it I-subject and I-imperson, that which is present when I-dream subject or I-person and its object find their synthesis.

All these names, images, are descriptions, devised to the end that one or other may open the way to the apprehension of the vital synthesis itself. But if we have understood at last—what could be clearer or more literal than just "the whole mind" as compared with its "halves," non-dual mind as the "father" of dual, undivided mind which we know only in the divided state by the comparison of opposites and complementaries?

11

Two Is One

TWO: So I can only use half a mind at any one time, one half and then the other. But I ought to be able to use the two together? Am I home?

ONE: You are separated from home by a thousand million miles, and as many incarnations.

TWO: Woe is me! How so?

ONE: *Who* is using *what?*

TWO: Hell's bells, I forgot! There is no one to use anything!

ONE: There is using, but no user and nothing used.

TWO: Be a good chap and put me right.

ONE: As a good chap you shall put yourself right.

TWO: I *am* half a mind every time I think or act, one half or the other, never the two together—because the thinking apparatus cannot do it.

ONE: You understand: go on.

TWO: But a sage *is* whole-mind. We recognise him as a sage precisely because he has apprehended the fact that he is "that." And he has been able to become that because he has come to know that he is not a person but imperson.

ONE: There was no becoming: nothing becomes what it is. But you could hardly say it less inaccurately in dualistic language.

TWO: But can a sage use his whole-mind in daily life?

ONE: If "he" is trying to "use" "his" mind it is not whole, for he still thinks he is a person: therefore he cannot.

TWO: Too bad! So how does he get out of that hat?

ONE: He is whole-mind, but he cannot "use" it in daily life, because in daily life all ways of using mind are dualistic.

TWO: Then how does he work?

ONE: When he works—to use your elegant expression— he does so as you and I do.

TWO: He re-becomes a person?

ONE: Precisely no—for he never was a person; nor were we.

TWO: So he just acts as though he were?

ONE: Like you do.

TWO: No difference?

ONE: Yes, an essential difference. He knows what he has to do, and what he is doing.

TWO: And I cannot?

ONE: You could, but you don't. He lives in the present: you live in the past and the future. He does what he does, while you dream, discriminate and judge.

TWO: He knows it is a doing, whereas I think I am doing it?

ONE: So that, though his words and actions are in duality, his mind remains whole.

TWO: Sounds gymnastic to me.

ONE: Why? Have we not understood that one is potentially two, and two potentially one?

TWO: Then we too, though dual, are one, and he, though one, is dual?

ONE: Of course, of course!

TWO: We are all one, though dual?

ONE: Of course, of C-o-u-r-s-e!

TWO: Then what is stopping me from knowing that I am One?

ONE: Your incorrigible asininity, nothing else.

TWO: Which quality the gentle ass himself entirely lacks?

ONE: Entirely. The mind that he is, though simple, is whole.

TWO: Why is it simple?

ONE: The apparatus has not yet developed the faculty of making concepts.

TWO: As a child's has not. That is why we must become "as little children"?

ONE: Very little ones: complexity, and its results, come quickly.

TWO: Whole-mind and its potential halves, its inherent

halves; half-minds and their essential, potential, inherent oneness! How damned simple it seems to be!

ONE: How many times? . . .

TWO: But why not realise it?

ONE: It is waiting for apprehension.

TWO: Yes, but *non-intellectual* apprehension.

ONE: That is so.

TWO: And that we cannot have as long as we . . . as long as we . . . how shall I put it?

ONE: Go on and on using our split minds in the weaving of unending and futile phantasies and judgments. Even light needs an aperture in order to reach a retina.

TWO: Enough to make anyone despair! What is the good of understanding all this?

ONE: This: you have learned at last to look in the right direction, but, in order to see, you still have to open your eyes.

TWO: And to realise that I haven't got any?

ONE: Nor anything else. And because there is nobody to look—know that there is a looking, which is whole-mind. Since nothing else is, that is your reality, and say, with a voice that makes the welkin ring—I AM.

12

Karuna: A Reminder

The great master of modern Japanese Zen ends the little book in which he speaks to us most directly, most profoundly and most frankly, with the following words. Speaking of the ko-an practice he says, "But there is one thing which requires a full recognition. . . . This is to remember that each ko-an is an expression of the Great Intelligence *(mahaprajna)* and that every such expression *gains significance only* when it is associated with the Great Compassion *(mahakaruna)*." The ko-an is a way of understanding like, though also unlike, any other; and the underlining of the three words is my doing—for without emphasis the statement might pass unnoticed despite its position among the last words of a very special book.

Every expression of pure cognition *(prajna)* "gains significance only," i.e. is *effective* only, when it is associated with pure affectivity *(karuna)*. That duality cannot find its synthesis unless each "half of the pair" is in mutual association. This need has been pointed out already (*One Half of a Pair,* Ch. 107). Let us point it out once more. Zen is very intellectual in its approach. "The fact is undeniable that there are more genuine and practically-working cases of satori among lay devotees of Shin than in the equivalent Zen circles. This is principally due, I think, to the absence in Shin of the ko-an methodology. Shin devotees are not generally so learned or intellectually inclined."

Is affectivity not treated in the West as a poor relation of understanding, as an obscure hanger-on of *prajna,* who, as such, can be ignored? But karuna, the synthesis of love-and-hate, is not poor, nor can it be ignored with impunity. On the contrary it is as noble and powerful as the synthesis of understanding and ignorance, and the two must stand hand-in-hand before the altar if they are to be united in a Hymen that *death shall not part.*

13

The Essential Explanation - IV: Reunion of Mind

If you stop thinking you stop using a split mind. If your mind is not split it is whole.

Seize it? No, you cannot. There is no you to do it, and a part cannot seize its whole. Nor, when you stop thinking, does the whole replace the halves that are not functioning. There is no displacement, no replacement, for that which functions is whole-mind, whether its dual aspect is apparent or not, for its functioning is theirs.

This is the explanation of Huang Po's statement that by a perception, sudden as blinking, that subject and object are one you will awaken to the truth of Zen—for awakening is precisely the reunion of the two parts of mind.

The Essential Explanation - V

If one really has an insight into the truth that there is no entity and no thing anywhere at all, then one no longer exists, and one is.

14

False Premises

What has been called Transvaluation of Values is a formal way of saying that we must clear out all the naïve and inadequate ways we have inherited of trying to explain what we have not understood.

We have not understood precisely on account of these half-baked notions which are based on false premises and which lack a dimension.

Whichever way we may turn we are faced with them, to such an extent that we may in general suspect that however we have been looking at a problem it is almost certain to have been wrongly envisaged.

It will be found that the majority of our troubles are due to this factor—that the problems themselves, as posed, are based on false premises.

Obiter Dicta

"Never allow yourselves to mistake outward appearance for reality.

"Avoid the error of thinking in terms of past, present and future. The past has not gone; the present is a fleeting moment; the future is not yet to come."

At the end of the *Wan Ling Record,* this looks like Huang Po's final advice to us, and it has all the qualities of that.

I think some of us find ourselves conforming with the first requirement to a considerable extent at least.

But the second? Do we do it at all? Are we even able to do it, conditioned from birth to the opposite? We may know it, we may believe it, we may see clearly how it is so. But actually to avoid thinking in terms of past, present and future? . . .

As individuals I do not think that we can, or ever could. Split minds are in subjection to time. But are we individuals? Both injunctions are addressed to whole-mind.

Attaboy!

15

Mind and Matter - II: Restatement

Can "matter" be affected by "mind"? The question is absurd, a naïve question based on false premises.

Whole-mind is manifest both psychically and materially, which manifestations form a pair of complementary dualities.

Split mind belongs to the psychic aspect of whole-mind, and a body is its complementary manifestation.

Split mind is a temporal phenomenon (subject to seriality), and its apparent function is the interpretation of whole-mind as manifestation. It is therefore whole-mind perceiving itself via its projection in duality.

Complementaries cannot, by their nature, affect one another, for they are not independent. Whichever acts does so as part of a whole. Therefore split mind and body cannot interfere with one another; nor can the psychic and material aspects of whole-mind.

It does not appear, therefore, that any kind of "organic" interference can occur between split mind and body, but "functional" only, except via the psychic aspect of whole-mind itself.

Matter is split mind's temporal interpretation of whole-mind in manifestation. It is therefore whole-mind perceiving itself via the dual projection of itself.

Split mind can mould and fashion matter via its body-object, but it cannot directly affect its own object-interpretation when that is dualistic, i.e. is the result of its own dichotomy. Matter can only be organically affected "upstream" of that dichotomy, that is, by the psychic aspect of whole-mind itself.

The reality of matter is its suchness only, the appearance of matter is a dualistic interpretation. Its suchness, being real, is immutable: its interpretation can only be affected by the parent of split mind and its object, i.e. by "the Father" (Imperson). See Table.

This interpretation, expressed diagramatically, will be seen to correspond with the Table called *Metaphysical Analysis of What We Are*, Ch. 81.

This is no accident. The items are themselves ultimately the same in each Table. Whole-mind is Unself (I-Reality), the Psychic Sphere is Imperson (I-subject, etc.), Divided mind is the Dividual (I-dream-subject, etc.), all three being degrees of subjectivity, and material things their apparent objects. The diagram is applicable to all manifestation in so far as it may express what we can know as truth.

The "action" (apparent action) of whole-mind is of another nature, for it is relatively real. But it cannot be used: it "uses" us—in a sense at least. As an object it is merely a concept like another, and impotent as such: as subject it is what we are in reality. It is what we find that we are when we awaken. Its apparent actions are in accordance with cosmic necessity. It is omnipotent, which does not mean that it has, or could satisfy, whims, which is our naïve notion of what we call "free-will," but merely that its potentiality is unlimited.

The whole question, therefore, as usually envisaged, is misconceived, and can never find an answer until it is correctly posed.

Diagram of Mind and Matter

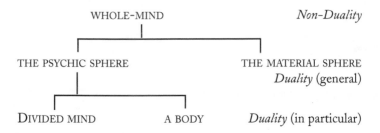

Reference to the Diagram called *Metaphysical Analysis of What We Are,* Ch. 81, will show the correspondences.

WHOLE-MIND equates with I-Reality, Unself, the Absolute, Brahman, Godhead etc.;

THE PSYCHIC SPHERE with Imperson, I-Subject, Observing Consciousness, The Father, The Buddhamind, The Original mind, etc.;

DIVIDED MIND with The Dividual, I-dream-subject, I-person, etc.;

THE MATERIAL SPHERE with All Objects;

A BODY with One Object.

As in the former Table, a multidimensional reality is here represented in a two-dimensional diagram, for Whole-mind is present in (or "behind") all three degrees of subjectivity, and A Body in its particular aspect belongs at the same time to The Material Sphere.

16

The Mechanism of Psycho-Kinetic Phenomena

If therefore there should be satisfactory evidence of

"matter" being directly acted upon by "mind" the explanation of such apparent action should be looked for "upstream" of the split mind, i.e. from a higher degree of subjectivity.

The perfection of this process is well-known through the Japanese masters of swordsmanship and archery, some of whom, with the help of Zen Masters and long years of training, succeeded in stilling the activities of split mind, and in relegating to abeyance all consciousness of self. Being in a state of total disponibility, their body and its acquired technique is at the disposal of impersonal consciousness (I-subject) which, unfettered by the apparent limitations of time and space, can act with im-mediacy, so that reaction accompanies action, subject and object become one, and, without desire of conquest or awareness of superiority, absolute success becomes automatic and inevitable.

That the elements of this process, in an embryonic form, are used unconsciously to a small extent by certain artists of all categories, and others in daily life, seems to be probable. It no doubt explains the phenomena in question. But, deliberately, consciously, to bring it to pass, that is, to enjoy the state of pure awareness and disponibility, is long and difficult indeed for humanity conditioned from birth as ours is to-day, for consciousness of self, and belief in the real existence of such, is an absolute barrier in the path, and the Way, as it is called, for "This" only lies open when that barrier is removed. Moreover it is only possible in the total absence of observation and reasoning. It is in the highest degree unlikely that any ordinary, or even extraordinary, person could know it, least of all consciously or with deliberation.

There may also be a pseudo-phenomenon which superficially resembles the one in question, and which is due to temporary alteration in the normal interpretation by split mind of a perception. This "illusion" or "hallucination" has never

193

been accorded any metaphysical significance.

17

Understanding of Zen: The Key that Is The Way

The Zen Masters did not speak very clearly; at least in surviving records logical discourse is rare. There are several reasons for this.

Zen was from the first a "secret" doctrine; it was a direct transmission "from mind to mind" "outside the scriptures."

It has always been a doctrine within the intellectual reach of a minority only; for the simple-minded there was the efficacious doctrine of the Pure Land of Amida Buddha.

Had it been clearly and publicly preached it would have excited ridicule among those incapable of understanding it, and mockery is "losing face," of which the oriental has a particular dislike. That may indeed seem odd for a Buddhist, since he cannot lose his "original face," and, in order to see that, which is his aim, he has to get rid of his apparent one—in fact he needs to lose his face in order to find it. However. . . .

Much of the apparent obscurity of Zen is due to the simple fact that the Masters are speaking directly to whole-mind, whereas we have been endeavouring to understand them in the contexts of split mind. The Masters sought to manœuvre their pupils into seeing the truth for themselves, rather than by explaining it to them in plain language, as far as that could be done, and to that end they had to address themselves directly to whole-mind and not to its dual aspects.

At first sight this explanation may seem too simple, but few obscurities will remain in the interpretation of the words of the Masters when this is realised. Really they speak "from mind to mind," from their realised satori to the unrealised satori of their pupils, seeking to open the way thereby for it to come into its own. And divided mind can only understand what they mean when it has come to understand the mind that is revealed by the resolution of its own apparent duality, that is, when it has ceased to be itself. That, you may say, is impossible, since parts cannot grasp their whole? No doubt. But whole-mind and its duality are one in two and two in one—as Professor Suzuki has told us. Perhaps that too is a ko-an? If so—try it: it is an easy one!

This applies to a considerable extent even to our own modern Western writings, though at a second degree, for ultimately they are often reflections of the words of the Masters. Our intuitions also, when they are real, come from undivided mind and are put into words, as well as may be, under the dualism of mind that is divided. And in re-reading our interpretation of these same intuitions we ourselves may have difficulty in following them, for we too may still seek to understand them according to the familiar modes of split mind.

For instance the I-concept is clearly inexistent in whole-mind, and an intuition therefrom will not contain any trace of it; but in the universe created by the interpretations of divided mind it is apparently not only existing but is an essential factor in our living.

When the Buddha adjures us on no account to cherish the notion of the existence of such a thing he is really adjuring us to abandon split mind and to seek mind "upstream" of bifurcation. Almost the whole of the Diamond Sutra is in this pattern, and becomes clear when this is understood, and it applies probably to all the *mondo,* indeed to nearly all the recorded words of the Masters, save those of Huang Po, Hui Hai, and such documents as the letter of Takuan to Yagyu

Tajima no kami Munenori.

It would seem to be essential, therefore, to urge pilgrims towards whole-mind, and, when they have understood, they will recognise that such intuitions are true therein, and that their apparent obscurity, as interpreted by split mind, is in fact the inevitable falsity inherent in seriality of vision.

But can we in fact, you are sure to ask, use whole-mind? This is probably a question based on false premises, like all the rest, to which an affirmative and a negative answer will both be true and both be false. We certainly cannot "use" it; there is neither a "we," as such, nor an "it." On the other hand we cannot not-use it, for divided mind as-a-whole is it. As "it," it is an object and inexistent, as "we" are, but as consciousness it is eternal and infinite, which to split mind is seen as continuous and ubiquitous. Moreover whole-mind is all that we are. As such we cannot not-know it, and we cannot not-use it—though there is nothing that can be known nor anything that can be used.

Therefore a "knowing," which is a "being," is inevitable, though only to the awakened may communication of such knowing be possible in any other form than that of an attempted interpretation of an intuition. The Sages can know split mind as a whole and divided, while we, subject to the I-concept, can only know split mind as a duality. We may not be able to know and to use mind made whole, but nothing can prevent us from being it and from knowing that we are. From that to living in it is only a step—or is it a leap? *"Gate, gate, paragate, parasamgate, Buddhi svaha."* *

---

* Colloquial translation: "Over, right over, beyond the beyond, beyond the behind, Awakening, what-ho!"

But is it "we" who leap? How could it be? That is surely a misleading image? There is a leaping, no doubt, but it is a no-leaping also. It is an abandonment rather than an undertaking, passive rather than active, surrender rather than attack. We have only to cease to recognise an illusory "us" in order to find that we are ourselves impersonal instead of personal. Why do "we" wait? Our impersonal reality is not waiting: it is functioning (in relative reality), and in so doing it is bringing us towards a state of disponibility. By recognising it as our wholeness we are making ourselves ready consciously to re-become it and to know ourselves absolutely as unselves.

Since awakening is essentially the wakening to whole-mind, and since the Masters addressed themselves directly to that, it is evident that not only can it be done but that such itself is the way to understanding. Whole-mind vision? Split-mind vision? That dual question is the key that is also the way.

18

Whole-Mind and the Way

The Sixth Patriarch (Hui Neng) stated his view of the self very clearly in the Platform Sutra, as clearly as, though with less emphasis than, that of the Buddha in the Diamond Sutra.

"He who is in the habit of looking down upon others has not got rid of the erroneous idea of a self, which indicates his lack of *Kung* (realisation of the Essence of Mind)," p. 43.

"When you get rid of the idea of a self and that of a being, Mount Meru will topple," p. 43.

"We should broaden our knowledge, so that we can know our own mind . . . get rid of the idea of 'self' and that of 'being,' and realise that up to the time when we attain Bodhi the 'true nature' is always immutable," p. 54.

"To believe in a self is the source of sin," p. 67.

"It is for the victims of ignorance, who identify the union of five skandhas as the 'self,' and regard all other things as 'not-self' (outer sense objects); who crave for individual existence and have an aversion to death without realising the hollowness of mundane existence, which is only a dream or an illusion . . . that the compassionate Buddha preached the real bliss of Nirvana," p. 80.

"And the so-called 'ego' arising from the union of these skandhas, together with all external objects and forms . . . are equally unreal, like a dream, or an illusion," p. 81.

If we find the Patriarch's approach confusing; if it is difficult for us to sort out from its total context, may we not recognise that this notion of self is half mind's interpretation of subjectivity in the seriality of time? Viewed in whole-mind it would clearly be seen as a *mis*-interpretation.

The Masters spoke from whole-mind for our good. Let us co-operate by also understanding in whole-mind—for that was what they asked of us. Their aim was to open us to whole-mind, and the way was to by-pass the delusive activities of divided mind so that we might have deliverance.

19

The "Doctrine" of Subjectivity

I am subjectivity only. I *am,* and nothing else whatever. And there is nothing else whatever. That is the "doctrine" of subjectivity.

But, in order to understand what *we are,* we are obliged to envisage subjectivity in three degrees, just as we find it necessary to give a label to everything we recognise and thereby to create apparent and illusory entities—*la distribution de marques d'identité aux fantômes!*

Subjectivity, at whatever apparent degree of limitation, is always nevertheless entire and "pure," i.e. immutable: its limitation lies in its apprehension and not in that which is partially apprehended, for the apprehending alone exists.

The first degree of apparent limitation of subjectivity is represented by bifurcation into subject and objects, such objects being the projection of subject and what we perceive as the world and everything therein. This is known as relative reality.

The second degree of apparent limitation of subjectivity is represented by the further bifurcation of subject into the subject of an individualised object with which it identifies itself, thereby "creating" the supposed individual entity. This has been called "personal subject," also "I-dream subject," but its only real existence lies in its basic subjectivity; as identified with its object it is illusory, then it belongs to the category of dreams, hallucinations, mental images of all kinds whether regarded as "waking," "sleeping" or "unconscious."

This second bifurcation need not be regarded as independent of the first, but can be seen as a secondary interpretation thereof, or as a lateral interpretation. The manner of regarding this does not seem to matter and is just a question of convenience.

The aim of this "doctrine"—which is no more a doctrine than any other, and which is neither more nor less real in itself than any other—is to enable us to understand the unreality of the supposed individual "self," which is thereby revealed as a misinterpretation, due to the identification of limited subjectivity with an object, subjectivity so conceived being necessarily thereby itself an object and so no longer subject *at all.* This disposes of the unique barrier that lies between us as subject and our realisation of that essential subjectivity.

This being understood, personal subject and the object with which it is identified no longer seem to exist for us, and we find ourselves the impersonal subject we always were, are, and for ever will be.

20

The Binocular Aspect of Subjectivity

What we call relative reality is the objectivity of *impersonal* subject. The reality of all objects sensorially perceptible lies in their subjectivity.

The objects of *personal* subject are purely psychic and are confined to the psyche in which that personal aspect of subjectivity is limited.

Both, as we know them, are interpretations by divided mind of apparent manifestations of whole-mind, the one general, the other particular. They represent two degrees of relative reality.

Each individual, as an object appearing in consciousness, is at the same time an object of impersonal, and an object of personal, subject—as we might say, "as he is" and "as he appears to *you.*"

This is clear in the case of "I am," which is pure subjectivity and reality speaking, whereas with any attribute, any adjective, the speaker thereby becomes the limited subject, interpreted and perceived as an object. "I am tall, or dark, or John, or angry" is a description of an object pretending to describe itself: subject is projecting an object and identifying itself with that object—which is dream or illusion and not relative reality.

Subject alone is real. All objects are concepts in split mind. It can readily be seen that no object can have a "self," and that the concept of an entity is senseless, for subject so regarded thereby becomes an object—which is identification (all identification being necessarily "false," the usual adjective is superfluous).

Every apparent object exists in mind only, i.e. is a projection of impersonal subjectivity, but it is perceived by personal subjectivity externalised as an object.

Personal subject cannot affect it because personal subject is itself identified with an object (a "person"), and an object cannot affect an object, but impersonal subject (Creator) can affect its own project (creation).

But do not let us forget that there are not really two processes, even simultaneous, though they must seem so to us viewed serially. Subject projects a world discretely (projects and re-projects every instant in the apparent sequence of time), and subject limited by dualism, bifurcated subject, the personalised aspect of that bifurcated subject, perceives it as an object external to itself.

21

Realisation

We are surrounded from birth to death with objects of all sorts and kinds, and we assume that they are all independent, existing in space and time, things-in-themselves, unconnected with one another and with ourselves. And when the Sages tell us that this cannot be so we are amazed and are unable to understand what they mean. Yet we recognise them as objects, and we surely know that an object cannot be such without a subject?

What, then, is the subject in question? No doubt the subject implied in ordinary language is the subject whose senses perceive the objects. This is sound enough, for so indeed it is, but we proceed to misinterpret this observation. For we imagine that the subject whose senses perceive objects is a body, which itself is an object like the others, and, like the others, apparently independent, existing in space and time, a thing-in-itself, unconnected with other objects.

When this false identification is removed we immediately understand that the subject in question is the subject of the body as well as of all other objects. This we have called Impersonal Subject, and it is our reality, all that we are, for objects, including the body and the divided mind that is an aspect of it, only exist as the objectivisation of that Subject. The object, the psyche-soma, to which we have attributed subjectivity, is impotent directly to affect other objects, whereas real Subject is omnipotent in relation to Its objects which are projections of Itself.

This error is the mechanism of our bondage. The way of liberation is awareness of the impersonal subject of all objects, awareness that we ourselves are that only, and that all objects, including the psyche-soma whose sensorial apparatus we operate, are projections, impotent to "do" anything whatever of their own initiative, entirely interdependent, and operable only by Impersonal Subject Itself.

This impersonal subject is whole-mind. It is immutable, never absent, never either active or quiescent. It is us whether we appear to be asleep or awake. It is the reality of every perception, the suchness of everything that appears to exist. It is also Consciousness—for all these words are just attempts on our part, attempts via divided mind to comprehend our reality. Our reality, however, cannot be comprehended, cannot be known as an object—since it is pure subjectivity—but when we realise that nothing objective is real we become aware that that which remains is *real*ity, and that we must be that. This is the meaning of the term "*real*isation."

Envoi

Establishment
In Pure Consciousness
Is Perpetual and Universal
Benediction Inhaled and Exhaled
As the Air We Breathe

Index

Sentient Publications, LLC publishes books on cultural creativity, experimental education, transformative spirituality, holistic health, new science, and ecology, approached from an integral viewpoint. Our authors are intensely interested in exploring the nature of life from fresh perspectives, addressing life's great questions, and fostering the full expression of the human potential. Sentient Publication's books arise from the spirit of inquiry and the richness of the inherent dialogue between writer and reader.

We are very interested in hearing from our readers. To direct suggestions or comments to us, or to be added to our mailing list, please contact:

SENTIENT PUBLICATIONS, LLC
1113 Spruce Street
Boulder, CO 80302
303.443.2188
contact@sentientpublications.com
www.sentientpublications.com